# BIBLIOTHERAPY

## FOR CLASSROOM USE

Written and Illustrated by
Jan Grubb Philpot

Incentive Publications, Inc.
Nashville, Tennessee

*Illustrated by Jan Grubb Philpot*
*Cover by Kristy Jones*
*Edited by Leslie Britt*

Library of Congress Catalog Card Number: 96-78571
ISBN 0-86530-353-3



PRINTED IN THE UNITED STATES OF AMERICA

# Table of Contents

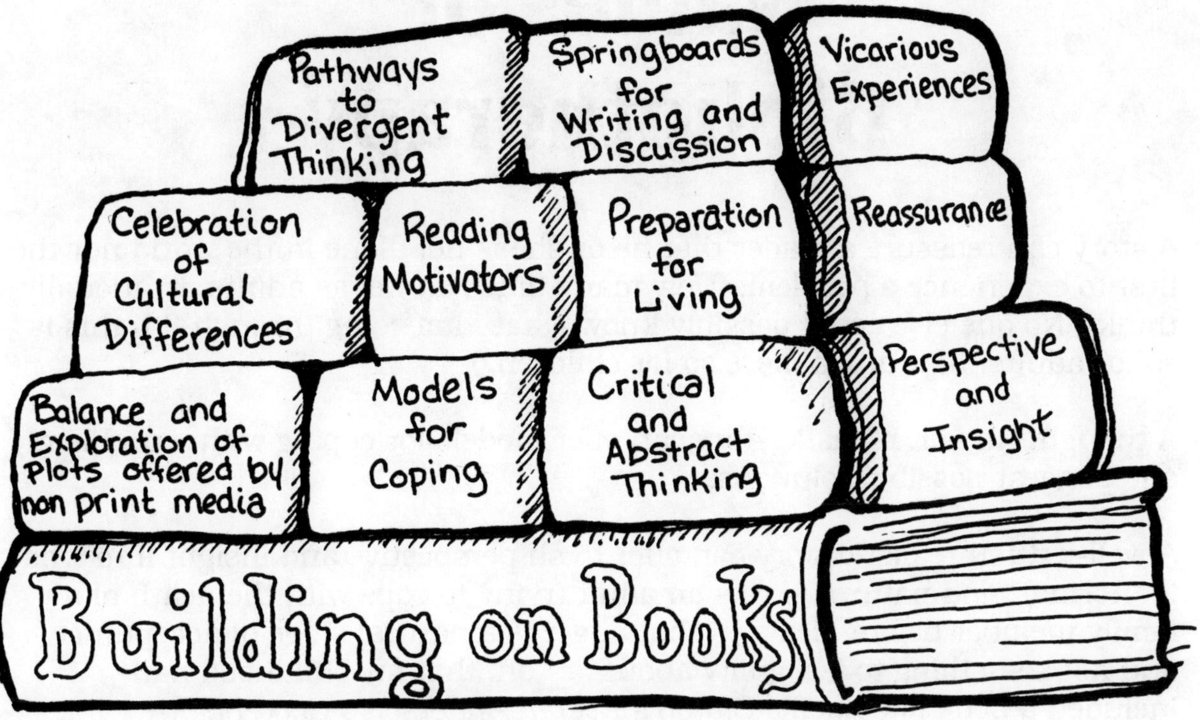


# Bibliotherapy

## *The "What?" and the "Why?"*

Bibliotherapy is a big word for a simple concept. It is the use of books to examine ourselves and gain insights that may help us live richer, more mentally healthy lives. Despite the use of that intimidating word *therapy*, bibliotherapy is not intended to be used in a clinical sense in the classroom. Knowledgeable educators can match individual students with books that can comfort and open doors for thought and discussion. This can be done on a classroom as well as individual level, with such books serving as motivators for reading and as launching pads for insightful writing, discussion, and creative endeavors.

Studies have shown that those children we recognize as "resilient," who weather life's storms and blossom into people with stable personalities, tend to be readers (Werner, 1984). The reader may search for a relevant book, be directed to one, or stumble upon one accidentally. However it happens, the rewards for individual students as well as entire classrooms are too valuable to be ignored.

# Values of Bibliotherapy

- A story can reassure a reader that he or she is not alone in the world nor the first to experience a problem. (How many times do we, as adults, irrationally think: "No one else could possibly know what I am going through"? If this is so for adults, how much more so for children?)

- A thoughtful, fair, realistic story can offer models for coping with a problem and suggest possible solutions.

- A well-written realistic story can offer fresh perspective and insight into what is "normal" and natural. (I was an adult trying to cope with the death of a family member before I learned that anger is a natural stage of acceptance and not something to feel guilty about . . . oh, that my childhood had included a book like Lucille Clifton's *Everett Anderson's Good-bye.*)

- A good realistic book offers valuable balance to what current media provides our children in daily doses. Consider the number of deaths and acts of violence a child experiences while playing a video game or witnesses in several hours of prime-time television viewing. These forms of media are, by nature, based on sheer entertainment value and bound by time limitations. Consequently, reasons, issues, aftereffects, and human pain are rarely explored. Not so in quality realistic fiction. The author takes time to develop a sensitive plot and provide insight into the characters. The theme is one of hope, not destruction.

- Realistic books are great reading motivators. Kids like to read about situations and characters they can identify with. As a middle school librarian, I am frequently asked, "Do you have a book about a kid my age?" Knowing these books is a great "secret weapon" in my goal to reach this particular age with books. Consistently, studies tell us that this is the age when even our better readers slack off. I can't resist telling a story about a fifth-grade girl I once dealt with. A quiet girl, she participated in activities and came willingly to the library with her friends, but she was a reluctant reader. One day, after hearing a series of book talks, she chose *The Pinballs* and kept it. Legitimately, of course. She just kept renewing it. In fact she kept the book renewed until the day she happily announced that I could have the book back now; she would be moving soon because she was being adopted. Unbeknownst to me, this girl was a foster child herself and obviously identified with Carly.

- The insight gained from realistic fiction (or nonfiction, for that matter) helps children gain other perspectives and deepens their compassion for the human condition simply because they are able to vicariously see the world through another's eyes and with another's problems.

- A realistic fiction book can serve to prepare for living and helps children "experience" emotions and situations they have not yet faced. Would we rather a child's first experience with a problem he or she is bound to face, such as death, be through a well-written book offering insights and hope or through blunt exposure to the real situation? When that experience comes, perhaps it could be somewhat comforting to already have a "frame of reference" and to remember having read about someone who felt as one feels and who coped in spite of it.

- Classroom usage of good realistic material can be particularly valuable. The divergent thinking that occurs in group follow-ups and discussions is often very special and helps students develop richer insights and a greater depth of meaning. Further, the use of topics relevant to today's world and today's kids prompts the kind of thinking and interaction that leads to motivated, self-directed projects and activities.

## To Remember —

Bibliotherapy, in short, is not just something to be considered for kids with problems. It is a way to match the right kid with the right book, promote critical and abstract thinking, foster moral development and problem solving, encourage discussion and compassion, celebrate culture and differences, motivate debate and creative endeavors, and provide springboards for high-quality writing experiences. This book is a small effort to furnish any librarian, teacher, or counselor with the resources and ideas to make bibliotherapy an integral part of their "bag of tools"!

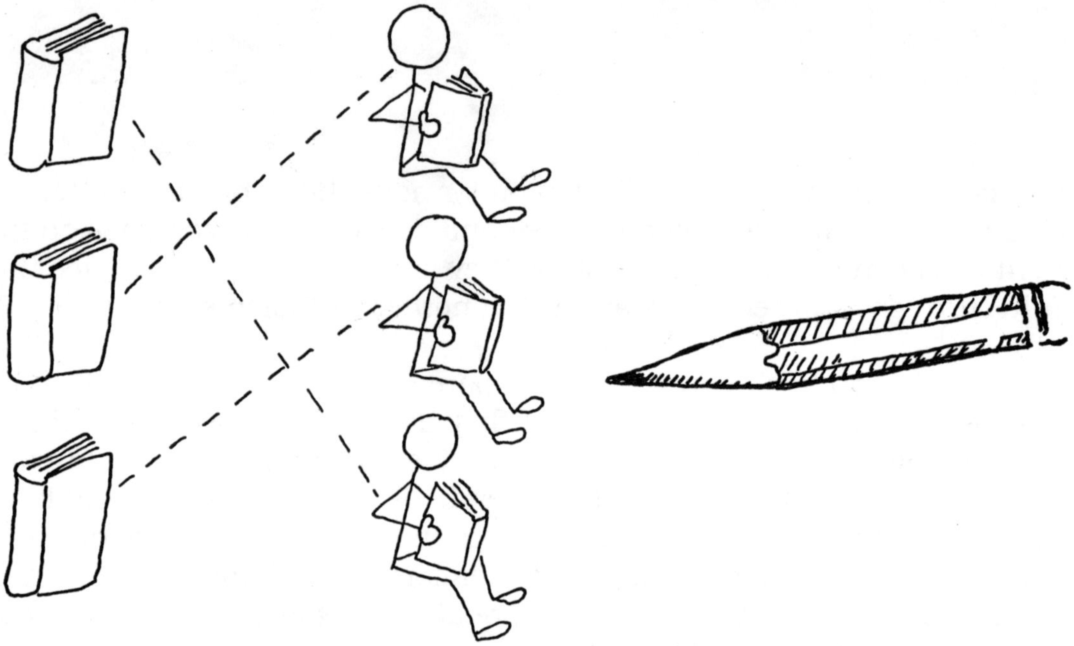

# Matching the Right Book with the Right Child

Matching the right book with the right reader at the right time is essentially what bibliotherapy is really all about. And remember . . . those books don't have to deal with problems . . . they can deal with interests. The idea is that reading builds problem-solving skills. If kids turn to books because of interest, they are a short step away from using reading for insight.

Knowing the books that are available is, of course, one aspect (and one reason for this resource!). Knowing one's readers is another. This is not difficult for self-contained classroom teachers whose time and interests are primarily focused on a single group. It does, however, pose more of a problem for teachers dealing with students only one period a day or for resource personnel seeing students only when they visit an office or a library. Most schools have worked out a system via counselors to let involved teachers know of a student crisis. However, as we have recognized, bibliotherapy isn't just for kids in a crisis, and it certainly does NOT take the place of counseling. Intuitive teachers will, of course, pick up on student interests and concerns via discussion and writing portfolio pieces, but this takes a bit of time. The following activities provide quick ways to learn about your students' interests on the first day, as well as "break the ice" and serve as good "getting to know you" sessions: 1) Me in a Nutshell, 2) R.E.A.D.E.R. Survey, and 3) a longer and more detailed Reader's Interest Inventory. Take your pick! Several ideas are given so that you can choose the one that best matches your classroom situation and middle school level. But all are designed for the same purpose: to provide you with a basis for beginning to match the right student with the right book.

# Me in a Nutshell

"Me in a Nutshell" is a simple get-acquainted activity. A great deal of information about a student can be gleaned from a few lines, and, in most cases, a teacher will immediately have an idea about the types of books that might interest a particular student, as well as relevant insight into that student's personality.

Use the master on the following page as a guide for students. The format for filling out the sheet is listed below:

Line One: first name
Line Two: adjective describing self
Line Three: adjective describing self
Line Four: "feeling" descriptor or statement
Line Five: statement
Line Six: family relationship (ex.: brother, sister, etc.); name
Line Seven: name of friend(s)
Line Eight: noun or statement
Line Nine: statement
Line Ten: statement
Line Eleven: statement
Line Twelve: statement
Line Thirteen: statement
Line Fourteen: last name

The simplicity of this activity is quite deceiving. For example, read about "Chris in a Nutshell" below:

Chris.
I'm a little bit funny,
And a whole lot energetic.
Most of the time I feel pretty good,
And I think a lot about basketball.
I'm the brother of Lon,
And the friend of Brandon.
I dislike writing poetry,
And I hope NEVER to have detention.
I'd like most of all to be able to draw,
And I wish I could see my dad more often.
Someday, maybe, I'll be a pilot.
Smith.

Right away, it is easy to guess that books about basketball, drawing, and pilots would probably interest Chris even if he is a reluctant reader. It would be a challenge to try to find poetry that might appeal to him and want to make him read more. Chris has given us other clues to his personality that might prove insightful later.

Hint: You might fill one of these out as well. Students will enjoy knowing a little more about their teacher!

__________________

I'm a little bit ____________ .

And a WHOLE LOT ____________ .

Most of the time I feel ____________ .

And I think a lot about ____________ .

I'm the ____________ of ____________ .

And the friend of ____________________ .

I dislike _________________________ ,

And I hope NEVER to _______________

________________________________ .

I'd like most of all _______________

____________________________ .

And I wish __________________

_______________________ .

Someday, maybe, ________

_____________________ .

And that's ME in a nutshell!

Student ______________________________

**R**EALLY LIKE TO READ *(TYPES OF MATERIAL)* ____________

______________________________

**E**NTHUSIASTIC ABOUT ______________________________

______________________________

**A** DREAM OF MINE IS TO ______________________________

______________________________

**D**EFINITELY INTERESTED IN ______________________________

______________________________

**E**XTRACURRICULAR ACTIVITIES INCLUDE ____________

______________________________

**R**ELEVANT INFORMATION NEEDED ABOUT ____________

______________________________

# What's Your Bag?

## *A Reader's Interest Inventory*

1. What do you like best to do in your spare time? ______________________
2. What hobbies do you enjoy? ______________________________________
3. What is your all-time favorite book? _____________________________
4. If you could visit any place in the world, where would it be? __________
5. What do you hope will be your career one day? _____________________
6. Do you prefer fiction or nonfiction books? __________________________
7. If you are interested in sports, which one interests you the most? ______
8. Do you collect anything? _____ If so, what do you collect? ____________
9. What subjects do you like best in school? __________________________
10. If you could meet any famous person (living or dead), who would it be? _____________________________
11. What is the title of the last book you read? _______________________
12. What types of books do you most enjoy? (Circle your responses.)

| | | |
|---|---|---|
| Fantasy | Realistic Stories | Sports |
| Biographies | Mysteries | Science Informational |
| Adventure | Science Fiction | Other: ______________ |
| Romance | Humorous Fiction | ____________________ |
| Poetry | How-to Books | ____________________ |
| Horror | Historical Fiction | ____________________ |

________________________________________________________________

________________________________________________________________

13. Does anyone in your family like to read? If so, who? _______________
14. What are a few topics you would like to know more about? ___________
15. What is something you do very well? _____________________________

# Building on What You Have Learned

Once you have completed at least one of the activities included in this section, you have probably gained some insight into the varied and diverse personalities and interests of your students. Those insights will serve you well in individualizing your curriculum, aiding students in adjustment, and in making each student feel as if you are truly interested in him or her as an individual. And, of course, you now have a good handle on where to start in matching the right book to the right child!

Don't let the opportunity go by to make at least one special effort this year to personally put a book into the hand of every single student who has shared what is "nearest and dearest" to them with you. Use the master on page 16 to keep track of your efforts to personally introduce a student to a book. If you are unable to think of or find a book you think would interest a particular student, use the form on page 17 to enlist your librarian's efforts. Write a short personal note on the top of the form on page 17 to the student explaining why you think he or she might enjoy the book and asking for a response to your selection. You won't win them all, but many reluctant readers have come to enjoy books through the personal interest of a teacher. Besides, all of your students will enjoy the warm feeling that comes from the extra attention of a teacher who takes the time to notice an individual student's interests and match those interests with a specially chosen book.

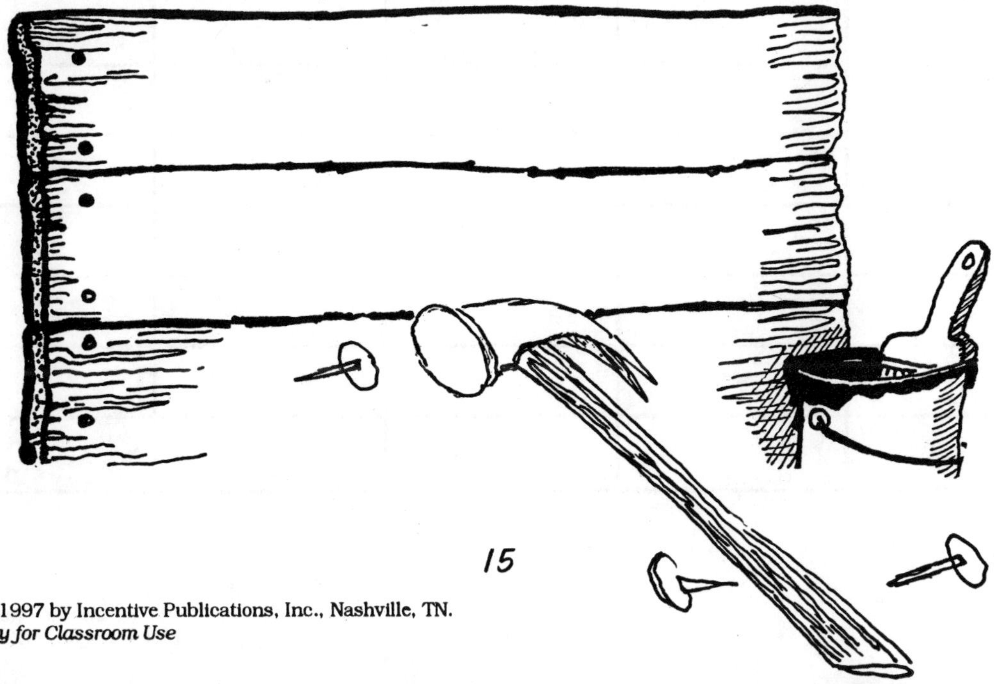

# Goal This Year:

## *Matching the Right Book to the Right Reader!*

| Student | Title recommended | Date recommended | Feedback | Follow-up ideas |
|---|---|---|---|---|
| | | | | |
| | | | | |
| | | | | |
| | | | | |
| | | | | |
| | | | | |
| | | | | |
| | | | | |
| | | | | |
| | | | | |
| | | | | |
| | | | | |
| | | | | |
| | | | | |
| | | | | |
| | | | | |
| | | | | |
| | | | | |

Every now and then you find something that seems like

# A Perfect Fit!

I thought you might like this book because . . .

(Please let me know if you liked it!)



# Help! I'm Stuck!

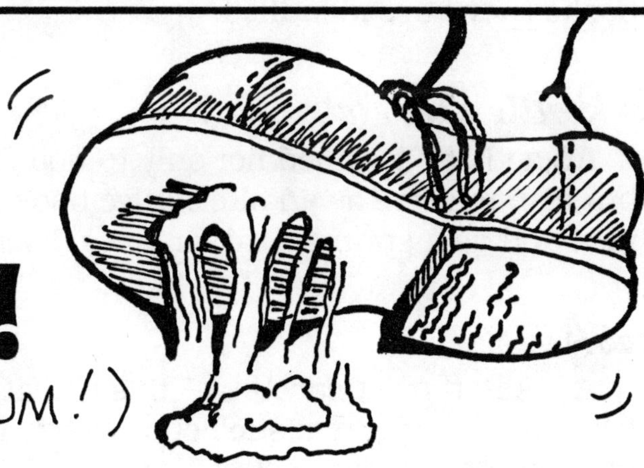

(BY GUM!)

Dear Librarian,

One of my goals this year is to match every reader in my classroom with just the "right book." However, I am having difficulty locating one for ______________________________. I would like to enlist your expertise in this area. I have attached a copy of this student's reading interest inventory. Please let me know of any suggestions you may have.

Thank you,

______________________

# Talking about . . . Realistic Fiction

The activities in the following section were designed to get kids interested in and talking about realistic fiction. Included in this section are:

### Realistic Fiction Role Play:

A participation activity designed for use in introducing students to this genre. The activity is a series of "mini–book talks" that may hook your students onto reading.

### The Top Ten:

This activity will give you some insight into the problems your students consider most important to their age group. It will have your students identifying the resources and materials their media center has to offer concerning these problems. Don't be surprised if you catch a few students checking out books they have identified.

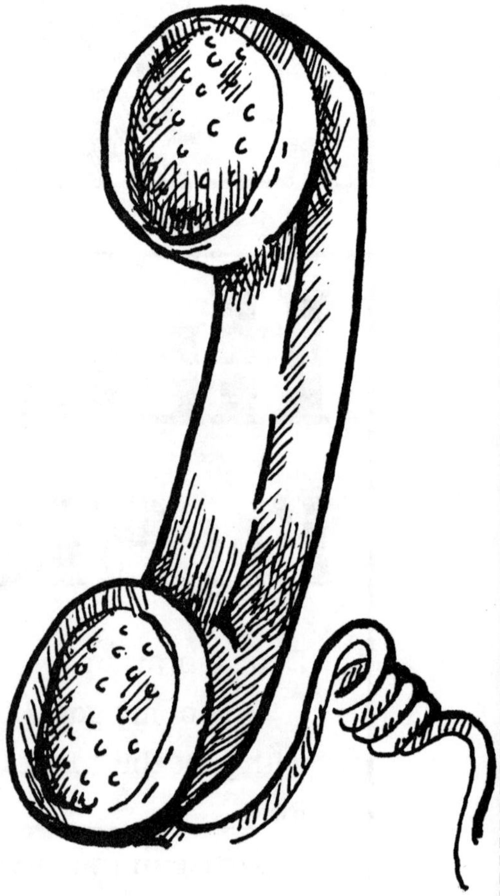

### The Reality Panel Talk Show:

An activity designed not only to hook readers, but also to serve as an alternative book reporting idea and as a springboard for class discussion.

### Dear Annie:

A take-off on "Dear Abby," this activity works best when a variety of realistic fiction books have been read by members of a class. It is a springboard for thought, discussion, and problem solving.

### The Pickle Jar:

This idea furnishes you not only with an ongoing display, but allows students who may be reluctant to share their concerns and provides them with an anonymous way to get a tip on a resource that may be helpful or comforting.

# Realistic Fiction Role Play

The following Realistic Fiction Role Play is an excellent way to introduce an audience to this genre. It is an entertaining and motivating activity that can be used by counselors, teachers, and librarians. A series of mini–book talks or "book hooks," this activity informs students of the many varied topics available in realistic juvenile fiction. Further, this activity lends insight to the value of such books.

To most effectively use this program, consider the steps listed below:

1) Duplicate the Realistic Fiction Role Play on pages 20–24. Cut apart the pieces and laminate; or, to make the sizes consistent, glue each to an index card and laminate.

2) Display the books used in the role play, as well as others tagged with their topic/theme (Divorce, Stepfamilies, Peer Problems, Death and Dying, etc.).

3) Pass out the laminated cards. You may choose to pass them out in the order the audience is seated. If, however, you choose to mix them up so that no one knows which member of the audience is to "pop up" next, you need to also make yourself a set of index cards with the numbers one through thirty-six written in large print. If this is the way you choose to conduct your role play, instruct the audience members to note the number on their piece and to speak when you display it.

4) Explain the role play to your audience. Explain that the dark italicized print in parentheses is what they are to do. The rest is what they will speak. Titles are to be read aloud as part of the script. These are italicized within the script.

5) Following your role play (wasn't that fun?), give your audience a copy of the bibliography of books (page 25) used in the role play. You might also duplicate the bibliographies found on pages 60-79 of this book for a wider selection on a greater number of topics. It would be helpful to at least have this available, even if you choose not to duplicate it for everyone. Now is also a good time to give some book talks on quality realistic fiction (see the book talk section, pages 27-33).

# Realistic Fiction Role Play

**1.** Ain't nobody understands me. Ain't nobody CARES!

**2.** ***(Patting previous speaker on the back)*** Fellah, I don't know where you been, but you just haven't met the right book yet.

**3.** ***(Sounding belligerent)*** Hey, I KNOW about books! That "happily ever after" business isn't the way life goes!

**4.** That's right, and what's some made-up character got to do with what's real and what's not anyway? It's not like they ever really lived what I live!

**5.** Like someone said, you just haven't met the right books . . . or maybe I should say the right characters.
And now . . . MAY I PRESENT . . . ONE OF THE GREATEST SECRETS ON EARTH! Yes, folks, you will laugh, you will cry, you will IDENTIFY! Presenting . . .

THE CAST OF REALISTIC FICTION!

**6.** ***(Screaming)*** WHY ARE YOU DOING THIS TO ME? WHY? THIS IS THE ABSOLUTE END OF THE WORLD!

**7.** ***(Patting previous speaker on the back)*** Ah, Karen, don't be so upset. *It's Not the End of the World.* I've been living with it for years. You'll get used to it. You know all those books about divorce? They're mostly for kids who are just starting it. There ought to be one about a kid who's lived with it for a long time. Then you'd see that we all survive it. By the way, I'm Rosie. I ride on *The Divorce Express.*

**8.** ***(Turning to the next person)*** What are you writing?

**9.** ***(Getting up and walking around the room, inspecting people closely and writing in a "pretend" journal)*** I'm taking notes on all these people sitting here. Because I've SEEN them and I want to REMEMBER them!

**10.** ***(Going over to last speaker and yanking the "pretend" journal from her hands)*** Let's see that! ***(Pretending to read)*** MAN WITH MISMATCHED SOCKS, DOUBLE CHIN, AND BALD HEAD. WOMAN WITH CROSSED EYES AND LONG NOSE. UGLY LITTLE BOY WHO KEEPS PICKING HIS NOSE WITH FAT MOTHER WITH BAD HAIRCUT.

**11.** Man, that's RUDE, Harriet! What if someone found that?

**12.** ***(Sounding snide)*** Just call her *"Harriet the Spy."*

**13.** ***(Jumping up and yelling angrily)*** Hey, it's not as rude as calling a fat person in your class a "smelly whale" and "*BLUBBER*"!

**14.** Who did that?

**15.** Oh, cut out your bickering. You should have some REAL problems. What if you were a foster kid, huh? And you had to live with a stupid woman who couldn't even read? HUH?

**16.** ***(Standing and facing last speaker)*** And that bit of whining comes to us from *The Great Gilly Hopkins*. I've had it just as rough as you have, you dork. Yeah, you're not the only foster kid in the world. We all get knocked around and can't help what happens to us. Know what I call us? *The Pinballs.*

**17.** ***(Sounding disgusted)*** I'm really tired of all this moaning. The rest of us kids have problems every day, you know. I mean, kids can have NORMAL, awful problems. The most terrible, horrible, dreadful, awful thing that could happen to me happened today in school . . . right in front of everybody . . . THE WHOLE CLASS . . . I . . . I . . . I THREW UP!

**18.** Not so much fun, huh, *Ramona*? Yeah, well, I bet your mom tucked you into bed when you got home, and took your temperature and asked if she could get you anything. Right? Well my mom NEVER pays any attention to ME. She's too busy going to meetings and trying to fix all the drug addicts in town. Dinky Hocker, her own daughter, might as well be a fly on the wall for all she notices! But I fixed HER the night she went to get her "Good Samaritan Award." She came out of that banquet and ALL OVER TOWN, I mean ALL OVER IT . . . on sidewalks, buildings, and curbstones was painted "*DINKY HOCKER SHOOTS SMACK!*" THAT got her attention!

**19.** ***(Sounding sad)*** Yeah, well . . . be glad you got a mother you can rile. Mine's dead. *There are Two Kinds of Terrible*, you know.

**20.** That's not as bad as having a mom who deserts you, just leaves you and your brothers and sisters in a strange parking lot in a strange town. What if you had to start walking on your own to try and find an aunt you don't even know, and sleep in the woods and state parks and abandoned houses on the way. Then when you get there, you find out nobody really wants you around. Some *Homecoming*.

**21.** OK, guys, these people are learning that characters in books have real problems. But they may be getting the wrong idea.

**22.** ***(Standing and speaking loudly)*** OK, listen up, folks! Nope, it didn't "turn out happily ever after" for most of these characters. But . . .

**23.** And that is an important "but"!

**24.** NONE of these problems were the end of the world!

**25.** That's right. Gilly didn't get her mom back. Neither did Carly.

**26.** Karen's parents still got the divorce.

**27.** Nothing could bring Robbie's mom back. She was dead.

**28.** But every single story had ONE thing in common.

**29.** ***(Standing and announcing clearly)*** HOPE!

**30.** Right! None of these stories were the end of the world!

**31.** As James Baldwin said, "You think your pain and your heartbreak are unprecedented in the history of the world, but then you read. It was books that taught me that the things that tormented me most were the very things that connected me with all the people who were alive, or who had ever been alive."

**32.** Yeah, and Nina Bawden says, "A writer is giving his readers a means to gain a hold on fate by showing them that they can trust their thoughts and their feelings, that they can have faith in themselves. He can also show them a bit of the world, the beginning of the path they have to tread; but the most important thing he has to offer is . . .

**33.** ". . . a little hope . . . and courage for the journey!"

**34.** ***(Clapping before speaking)*** WHEW! Such long-winded speakers! The key word, folks, is HOPE. A good realistic book offers HOPE!

**35.** ***(Clapping)*** You're quite a speaker yourself! ***(Turning to crowd)*** That's it! That's all the characters we have for you today . . . but there's LOTS more. Check out the library!

**36.** And now . . . before we get back to the librarian (or teacher, etc.), shall we give ALL these fine characters a big hand for their presentation today? ***(Clap and get crowd to clap with you.)***

# Realistic Fiction Role Play

## *Bibliography of Sources*

Blume, Judy. *Blubber.* New York: Bradbury Press, 1974. **(Peer Relations)**

Blume, Judy. *It's Not the End of the World.* New York: Bradbury Press, 1972. **(Divorce)**

Byars, Betsy. *The Pinballs.* New York: Harper & Row, 1977. **(Foster Children)**

Cleary, Beverly. *Ramona Series: Ramona the Pest.* New York: Morrow, 1968; *Beezus and Ramona.* New York: Morrow, 1955; *Ramona and Her Father.* New York: Morrow, 1977; *Ramona and Her Mother.* New York: Morrow, 1979; *Ramona, Forever.* New York: Morrow, 1984; *Ramona the Brave.* New York: Morrow, 1975. **(Family Life)**

Danziger, Paula. *The Divorce Express.* New York: Delacorte Press, 1982. **(Divorce)**

Fitzhugh, Louise. *Harriet the Spy.* New York: Harper & Row, 1964. **(Peer Relations)**

Kerr, M. E. *Dinky Hocker Shoots Smack.* New York: Harper & Row, 1972. **(Parent/Child Relationships)**

Mann, Peggy. *There Are Two Kinds of Terrible.* Garden City: New York: Doubleday, 1977. **(Death and Dying)**

Patterson, Katherine. *The Great Gilly Hopkins.* New York: Crowell, 1978. **(Foster Children)**

Voigt, Cynthia. *The Homecoming.* New York: Fawcett Juniper, 1981. **(Neglect; Homelessness)**

# Top Ten

Challenge time! The media center claims it has a book about almost anything and one to help with almost everything! List the "Top Ten" problems you think kids your age have. Then visit your school media center. See if you can match a book title with each problem!

| Problem | Title/Author |
|---|---|
| 1 | |
| 2 | |
| 3 | |
| 4 | |
| 5 | |
| 6 | |
| 7 | |
| 8 | |
| 9 | |
| 10 | |

# The Reality Panel Talk Show

## *The Reality Panel Talk Show serves a number of purposes:*

- It serves as an alternative book reporting method, fostering creativity in participants and sparking interest in listeners.
- It tends to foster group discussion and invites higher-order thinking and insight.
- Invariably, one of the "characters" in your talk show will strike a chord with a listener . . . another reader has been "hooked"!

# Here's How:

1. Assign a "book pair" to two students. Book pairs are listed on pages 32–33. The books identified as pairs revolve around similar themes, and the characters your students will be asked to role play in the Reality Panel Talk Show have dealt with similar problems, although their circumstances and their manner of dealing with those problems may be different (just like in real life). Explain to these students that they will be "role playing" the main character of the stories, so as they read they need to think about what it might be like to be this character. Several book pairs might be presented in one Talk Show, or this might be a weekly or monthly activity, each time featuring characters dealing with a different theme.

2. The Talk Show Host will need to read both books. He or she should make a list of ways the characters and their problems are both alike and different. From these observations, a list of questions can be designed. Explain to the host that it will be his or her job to draw as much information about the stories and plots as possible from the characters who have lived them. An example of a format that might be used is presented on pages 29–31.

3. Arrange a seating format similar to a real talk show and allow the students to "strut their stuff." Allow time for questions and discussion from the audience. Be sure to have available bibliographies listing other books that cover the discussed theme (see the bibliography section of this resource, pages 60–79).

# The Reality Panel

## A Show Sampler

Characters: Narrator
Izzy, of *Izzy, Willy-Nilly;* Atheneum, 1986.
Paul, of *Hang Tough, Paul Mather;* J. B. Lippincott Company, 1973.

Theme: Coping with illness and disabilities

Narrator: Good afternoon, ladies and gentlemen! And welcome to **The Reality Panel**! Our program today is about learning to live with, and coping in spite of, disabilities or illness. We have with us here today two very special guests: Paul Mather of *Hang Tough, Paul Mather* and Isobel Lingard, known to her friends as Izzy, of *Izzy, Willy-Nilly.*

***(Narrator turns to panelists)***

Narrator: Now, Izzy and Paul, each of you have had very different things happen to you that changed your lives. Will you please tell our viewing audience just what happened to each of you?

Izzy:

Paul:

Narrator: Those things must have changed your lives considerably. But to understand how much, please explain to our audience the kinds of things you enjoyed doing before your accident, Izzy, and your illness, Paul.

Izzy:

Paul:

Narrator: Both of you were athletes, so this certainly changed your expectations of what you could do physically. Can you tell us something about how your bodies were changed and what you realized you were no longer capable of doing?

Izzy:

Paul:

Narrator: Your families must have been quite worried about each of you while you were going through this. How were they supportive?

Izzy:

Paul:

Narrator: It's my understanding that quite often families, in wanting to help, may actually try to overprotect. Did either of you experience this?

Izzy:

Paul:

Narrator: What about your friends? Did you find any negative reactions? In what ways were some of them supportive?

Izzy:

Paul:

Narrator: You two must have had times when you just felt like giving up. Can you tell us about that?

Izzy:

Paul:

Narrator: You've told us that your lives definitely changed as a result of your situations. Were you able to find a way to still enjoy the things you did before, or did you find new interests?

Izzy:

Paul:

Narrator: Certainly none of this has been easy for either of you, but you seem to be strong characters who decided to face the truth and learn to live with it as positively as possible. What would you say is the character trait you have that has most helped you adjust?

Izzy:

Paul:

Narrator: What people around you have helped you most in adjusting, and what do you think it is about them that has been the most help?

Izzy:

Paul:

Narrator: Before we go, Izzy and Paul, there may be people out there who either have to face living with an illness or disability, or who know someone who does. What would you like to say to help them?

Izzy:

Paul:

Narrator: That's all for now, folks. We've talked with two very brave young people today who certainly had a message for all of us. We want to wish them well. Let's hear a big round of applause for Izzy and Paul!

# Book Pairs

The following are "book pairs" that are chosen for similarity in theme, as well as for differences that will make for a lively discussion of comparisons and contrasts.

Following each title is the name of the suggested character to be portrayed by a student during the role play. Complete bibliographic information can be found in the bibliography section of this resource, pages 60–79. Several "book pairs" might be interviewed in a talk show, or several talk shows might be held throughout the year, each relating to a particular theme as real talk shows do.

**Death and Dying:**

Hermes, Patricia. *You Shouldn't Have to Say Good-bye.* (Sarah)
Little, Jean. *Mama's Going to Buy You a Mockingbird.* (Jeremy)

**Divorce:**

Blume, Judy. *It's Not the End of the World.* (Karen)
Cleary, Beverly. *Dear Mr. Henshaw.* (Leigh)

**Foster Children:**

Byars, Betsy. *The Pinballs.* (Carly)
Patterson, Katherine. *The Great Gilly Hopkins.* (Gilly)

**Learning Disabilities:**

Greenwald, Sheila. *Will the Real Gertrude Hollings Please Stand Up?* (Gertrude)
Pevsner, Stella. *Keep Stompin' Till the Music Stops.* (Richard)

**Mental Retardation:**

Cleaver, Vera and Bill. *Me Too.* (Lydia)
Shyer, Marlene Fanta. *Welcome Home, Jellybean.* (Neil)

**Peer Pressure:**

Estes, Eleanor. *The Hundred Dresses.* (Wendy)
Mazer, Norma Fox. *Mrs. Fish, Ape, and Me, the Dump Queen.* (Joyce)

**Physical Disabilities:**

Garfield, James. *Follow My Leader.* (Jimmy)
Voigt, Cynthia. *Izzy, Willy-Nilly.* (Izzy)

**Stepfamilies:**

Park, Barbara. *My Mother Got Married (And Other Disasters).* (Charlie)
Smith, Doris Buchanan. *The First Hard Times.* (Ancil)

**Values/Conscience:**

Bauer, Marion Dane. *On My Honor.* (Joel)
Murphy, Jim. *Death Run.* (Brian)

# Dear Annie

"Dear Annie" is an activity that will definitely get kids thinking and talking about possible solutions to problems in plots of realistic fiction. A take-off on the familiar advice columnists in newspapers, the activity can be utilized in the classroom in several ways.

The activity is a perfect way to make sure students are paying attention when either a book is being read aloud in class or the entire class is reading a paperback copy of the same book. Halfway through the book, have everyone stop and write a letter to "Dear Annie," taking the viewpoint of the main character. Have class members exchange letters and reply as Annie. Compare the various solutions to the main character's problems that have been offered by class members. Continue reading the book and see if any of the students' solutions come close to the author's final resolution of plot.

If students are each reading different books, this activity will make a wonderful alternative book reporting method. As suggested, have each student write a "Dear Annie" letter, taking the perspective of the main character and outlining the problems the character faces. The student may then read the letter aloud to the class, and the class may brainstorm possible solutions to the character's problems. Following discussion by the class, the student may explain how the book actually ended.

# The Pickle Jar

This display is a way to share bibliographies of realistic fiction books with your students. Students can anonymously (if they wish), fill out a "pickle" (see page 36) with a topic that is pertinent to their interests, such as "peer pressure," "stepfamilies," "choices," etc. You may collect the "pickles" in a "pickle jar" and then duplicate pertinent bibliographies of suggested reading from the bibliography section of this resource beginning on page 60.

Duplicate on green paper, or color. Place where students can locate easily. They can write down topics they would like to read about, and you can provide a bibliography for them.

Using an opaque projector, enlarge the "pickle jar" and add to your display!

# Thinking It through with the Literature Connection!

The following activities are based on four realistic fiction books for young people. They are designed to encourage thought and group discussion and to serve as launching pads for writing and research projects. Although each was designed with a particular book in mind (noted at the top of each master), you will find that the activities are often thoroughly adaptable to many other books as well.

# Walk Two Moons

## by Sharon Creech

*Walk Two Moons* is the story of Salamanca, a thirteen-year-old girl who sets out on a journey from Ohio to Idaho with her grandparents. Along the way, she recounts the story of her friend Phoebe, and, as she tells the story, she begins to realize that the parallels between her life and that of her friend's cannot be ignored. *Walk Two Moons* is the story of a young girl's realization that beneath the bad is always good, that there are different ways of coping, that always a "picture" can be seen in different ways . . . depending upon in whose moccasins one is walking.

**About the author:**

Sharon Creech divides her time between England (where she teaches American and British literature), and a cottage on Lake Chautauqua in New York State. Her previous three novels were published in England. *Walk Two Moons* received the 1994 John Newbery Medal.

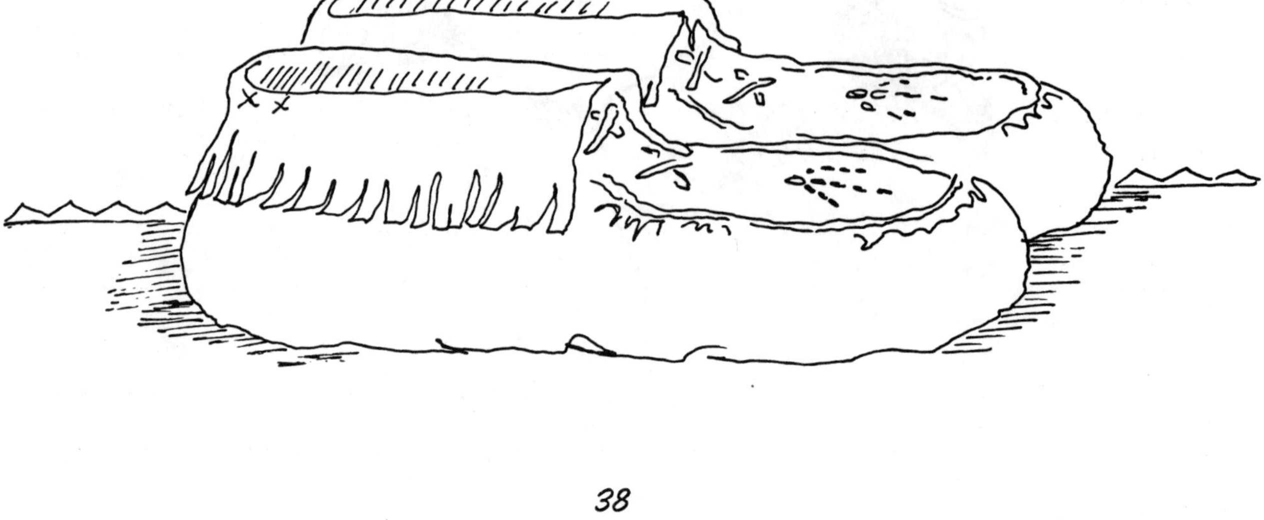

Creech, Sharon. *Walk Two Moons*. New York: HarperCollins, 1994.

Mrs. Partridge is the "mysterious visitor" who leaves messages on Peeby's porch. She thinks that the messages are "grandiful surprises" from which anyone can find meaning for his or her own life. Read again each of the messages Mrs. Partridge left. Decide how the messages apply to the events happening in the lives of the other book characters:

| Mrs. Partridge's message: | What the message means to a book character: |
|---|---|
| *Don't judge a man until you've walked two moons in his moccasins.* | |
| *Everyone has his own agenda.* | |
| *In the course of a lifetime, what does it matter?* | |
| *You can't keep the birds of sadness from flying over your head, but you can keep them from nesting in your hair.* | |
| *We never know the worth of water until the well is dry.* | |

Which of Mrs. Partridge's messages has special meaning to you? Write about the life event that you have experienced which relates to this message.

Creech, Sharon. *Walk Two Moons*. New York: HarperCollins, 1994.

# I'll Walk in Your Moccasins

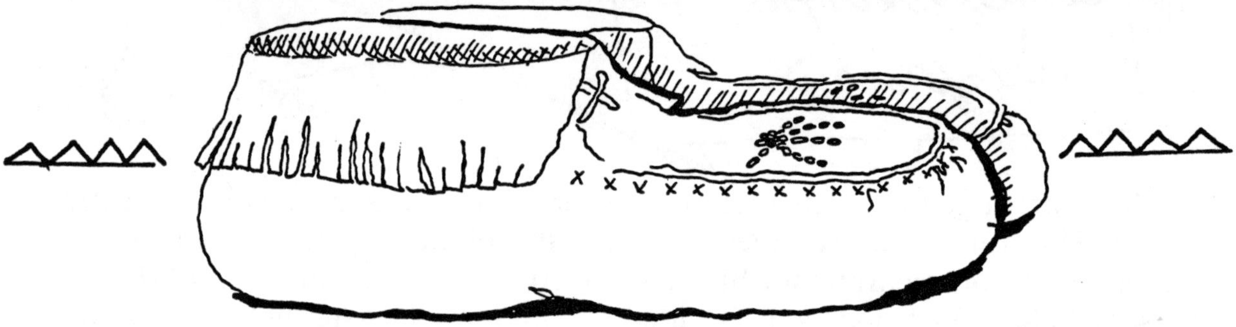

Gramps and Salamanca made up a game. They took turns pretending they were "walking in someone else's moccasins," and they told how they thought that person was feeling. Finish the beginnings of their "pretend" statements with feelings you think each character might have based on events in the book.

*If I were walking in Peeby's moccasins, I would* ______________________________

______________________________________________________________.

*If I were walking in Gramps' moccasins, I would* ______________________________

______________________________________________________________.

*If I were walking in Mrs. Cadaver's moccasins, I would* ________________________

______________________________________________________________.

*If I were walking in Salamanca's moccasins, I would* __________________________

______________________________________________________________.

Think of the names of three people in your world. Imagine for a moment that you "walked in their moccasins." Make "pretend" statements and think how you would feel if you were that person.

*If I were walking in* _______________*'s moccasins, I would* _______________

______________________________________________________________.

*If I were walking in* _______________*'s moccasins, I would* _______________

______________________________________________________________.

*If I were walking in* _______________*'s moccasins, I would* _______________

______________________________________________________________.

Creech, Sharon. *Walk Two Moons*. New York: HarperCollins, 1994.

# Green-Eyed Monsters

Salamanca discovered that beneath the events she could not accept and her bad behavior were jealousies. Most were foolish, she said, and one was not. Yet when she put herself in "another person's moccasins," she could better understand why things were not the way she wished they were. Write about Salamanca's feelings, and then contrast her feelings with those of a character "in another pair of moccasins." Use the back of this sheet if you need more room to write.

*Salamanca was jealous that Ben wrote about someone else in his journal. Why did Salamanca feel this way?*

______________________________________________

*What would be Ben's side of the story?* ______________________

______________________________________________

*Salamanca was jealous that her mother had wanted more children. Why do you think she felt this way?*

______________________________________________

*What did Salamanca decide must have been her mother's feelings?*

______________________________________________

*Salamanca was jealous that Peeby's mother came home while hers did not. She says this jealousy is not foolish and will not go away quickly. Why is it not foolish?*

______________________________________________

*What must Peeby have felt?* ______________________

______________________________________________

Compare your feelings about a situation in your own life with someone else's feelings about the same situation. Are they the same, or are they different? Walk two moons in each set of moccasins:

| My feelings: | __________'s feelings: |
| --- | --- |
| | |

Creech, Sharon. *Walk Two Moons.* New York: HarperCollins, 1994.

# Catching Fish in the Air

Salamanca came to realize that sometimes she "tried to catch fish in the air," meaning that she wanted to believe things that simply were not possible or true. She realized that other people did the same thing and that they did so to protect themselves from what was real.

How did Salamanca try to "catch fish in the air" in regard to her mother?

______________________________________________

______________________________________________

______________________________________________

How did Peeby try to "catch fish in the air" in regard to her mother?

______________________________________________

______________________________________________

______________________________________________

Have you ever tried to "catch fish in the air"? Tell about your fish: ________

______________________________________________

______________________________________________

Salamanca learned that trying to "catch fish in the air" is a normal and human thing to do. She learned that what was important was that one finally realizes the difference between fish in the air and what is truth . . . then tries to find the good parts in the "bad truth."

Once you realized that your "fish in the air" was just that, what good things did you find came with the "bad truth"?

______________________________________________

______________________________________________

______________________________________________

______________________________________________

Creech, Sharon. *Walk Two Moons*. New York: HarperCollins, 1994.

# Loss

The characters in this story each had to handle the loss of someone they loved in very different ways. Write how each person handled accepting death in the space below.

| Salamanca's father: |
|---|
| Gramps: |
| Salamanca: |

Have you ever lost someone very important to you, or a very special pet? Have you ever lost something else that meant a great deal to you, or had to move from a place you loved? In the first space below, write how you were able to accept what had happened. Then compare your situation with the reactions of others who lost the same person, place, or thing.

| |
|---|
| |
| |

Creech, Sharon. *Walk Two Moons.* New York: HarperCollins, 1994.

# Pandora's Box

Salamanca compared the bad events in life to Pandora's box. She decided that "bravery is looking Pandora's box full in the eye as best you can" and then turning to the good parts where the "smoothbeautiful folds are." Can you compare a bad event in your life to Pandora's box . . . and see both the bad and the "smoothbeautiful folds"?

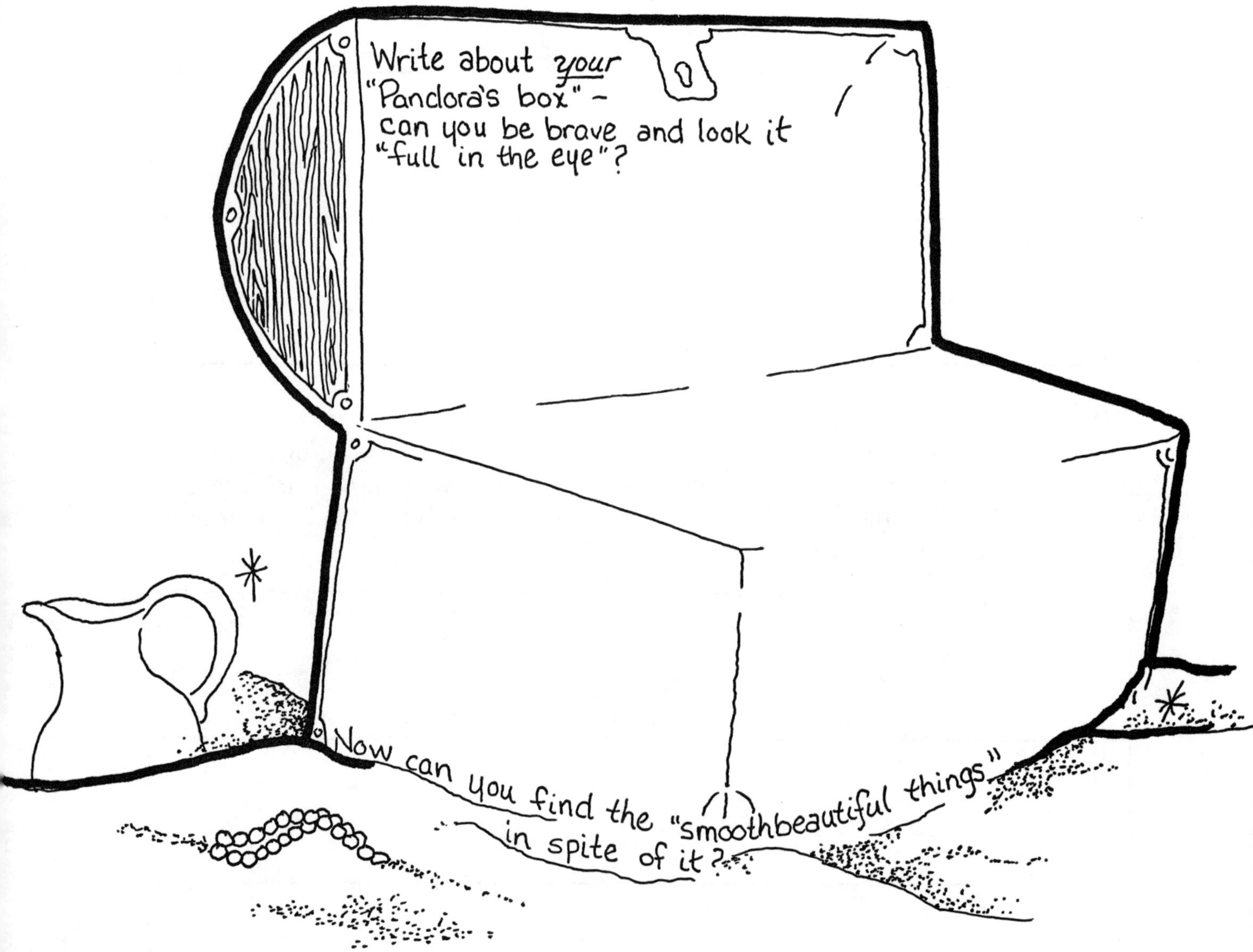

Creech, Sharon. *Walk Two Moons*. New York: HarperCollins, 1994.

# *More Things to Do with*
# Walk Two Moons . . .

Adages are wise sayings that often speak "volumes in a nutshell." Mrs. Partridge shared special adages in this story. Have the students share adages that they have heard at home and discuss the meanings of those sayings. Have them examine a reference book of quotes to find a special adage that has meaning to them and write about an event in their lives to which the adage applies.

Basic to the theme of *Walk Two Moons* is the concept that understanding the feelings of another is key to harmony inside oneself. Do a simple classroom exercise in listening and reflection of feeling to help students learn to communicate and empathize with others. Divide the class into partners. Explain that the partners will take turns listening very carefully to each other and reflecting back both what they have heard and what they think the speaker is feeling. The first person must tell the other of an event or problem about which they feel very strongly. The second person should summarize what they have heard, then add *"and I think you feel* ________________________________________ because ________________________________________. Is that right?" If the second person fails to understand what the speaker has said and is feeling, he must listen and try again until he understands.

Mr. Birkway showed Salamanca's class a picture that could be looked at in two ways. In one way, there are two people facing each other. In another way, the picture is a vase. He wanted the class to understand that people sometimes look at the "same picture," or event, in very different ways. Have your class brainstorm "pictures" (a ballgame, for example, with a winning side and a losing side) that can be seen in different ways, depending on who is looking.

# Dear Mr. Henshaw

## by Beverly Cleary

Leigh Botts spills his feelings in both his diary and the letters he writes to the famous author, Mr. Henshaw. As he writes, the reader experiences his growth in learning to cope with his parents' divorce, as well as with his feelings of alienation both from his father and from the students at school. *Dear Mr. Henshaw* received the 1984 John Newbery Award.

***About the author:***

Beverly Cleary is a prolific author of books for young people and is perhaps best known for her "Ramona" series. Her characters are loved because they have personalities and problems with which so many children can identify.

Cleary, Beverly. *Dear Mr. Henshaw*. New York: Dell, 1983.

# Growing Characters

When Leigh needed help writing a story for school, Mr. Henshaw advised him that a good character needed to solve a problem or change in some way. We all have problems, and in learning to cope in spite of them (or perhaps because of them!), we grow. Leigh knew this would make his story better.

In the end, Leigh grows, too. Consider how Leigh's attitude changes toward the different situations in his life throughout this book.

| Leigh's attitudes about: | How Leigh felt at first: | How Leigh felt later: | What events in the story help you know Leigh has changed? |
|---|---|---|---|
| School | | | |
| His father | | | |
| His parents' divorce | | | |
| Friends | | | |
| His lunchbox problem | | | |
| His chores at home | | | |

You may have grown in your attitudes about different situations, too. Think about it! Can you make a chart depicting your own growth?

Cleary, Beverly. *Dear Mr. Henshaw*. New York: Dell, 1983.

# How Well Do You and Your Parent Know Each Other?

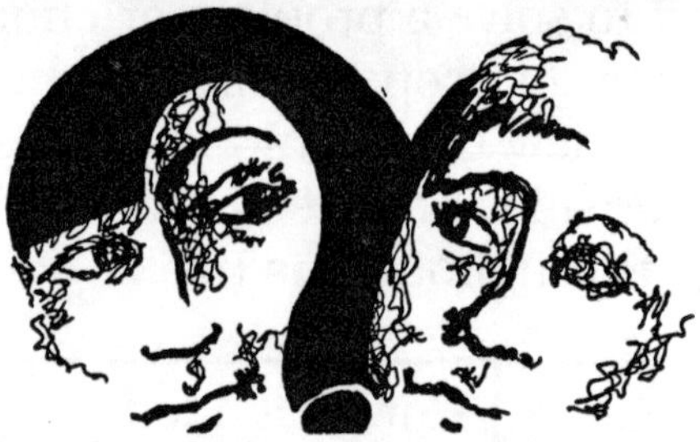

Leigh didn't feel that his father knew him very well. How well do you know your parents? How well do they know you? Fill out the top section of this sheet. Then cut off the bottom portion and ask one of your parents to fill it out. Get together and discuss the results. How well do you know each other?

## *I Think My Parent's . . .*

Favorite color is________. Biggest problem is ______________________________.

Favorite thing to do is __________________. Favorite food is _______________.

Favorite kind of music (or musical group) is _____________________________.

Favorite all-time movie is __________________. Best friend is ______________.

Favorite possession is __________________________________________________.

Greatest dream for the future is _____________________________________.

Biggest disappointment was ___________________________________________.

Best memory is of ______________________________________________________.

- - - - - - - - - - - - - - - - - - - - - - - - - - - - - - - - - - - - - - - -

## *I Think My Child's . . .*

Favorite color is________. Biggest problem is ______________________________.

Favorite thing to do is __________________. Favorite food is _______________.

Favorite kind of music (or musical group) is _____________________________.

Favorite all-time movie is __________________. Best friend is ______________.

Favorite possession is __________________________________________________.

Greatest dream for the future is _____________________________________.

Biggest disappointment was ___________________________________________.

Best memory is of ______________________________________________________.

Cleary, Beverly. *Dear Mr. Henshaw.* New York: Dell, 1983.

# One Step Closer!

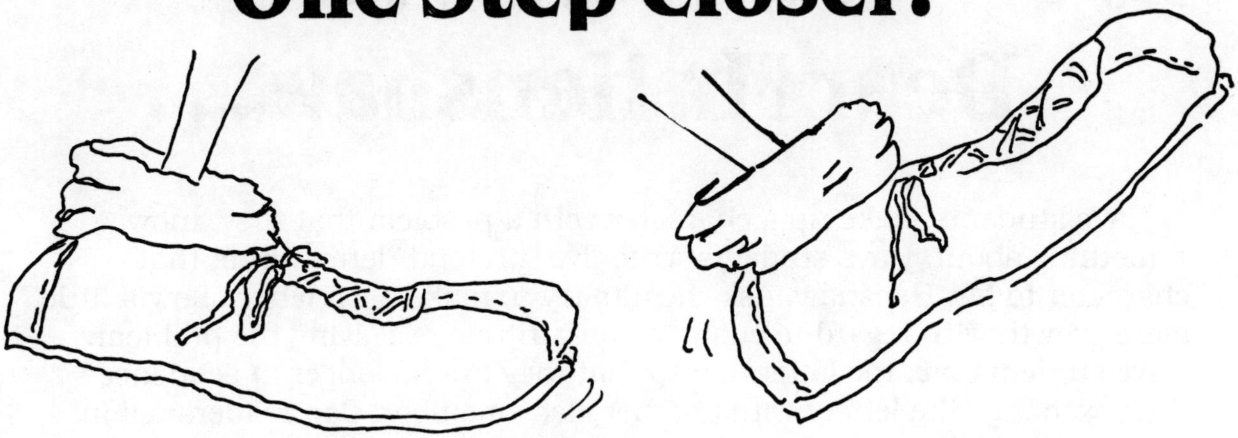

Leigh had a goal in this story. He wanted to become a writer. What were some of the steps he took to start working toward his goal?

| |
|---|
| 1. He wrote to a famous author and asked for advice. |
| 2. |
| 3. |
| 4. |
| 5. |
| Can you think of more? |

Think of a goal you would like to achieve. What are some of the steps you could take to reach it?

## *My Goal:* ______________________________

Things I can do now to help me achieve my goal:

| |
|---|
| 1. |
| 2. |
| 3. |
| 4. |
| 5. |

Can you think of more? Are you already doing some things that will help? What are they?

Cleary, Beverly. *Dear Mr. Henshaw.* New York: Dell, 1983.

## *Other Things to Do with*

# Dear Mr. Henshaw . . .

Have students make up a character with a problem that they know something about. Have students write five "pretend" letters from that character to Mr. Henshaw. Ask them to try to make each letter show a little more growth with regard to changing an attitude or solving the problem. Have students mix the letters up so that they are no longer in sequence, then exchange the letters with another class member. Can readers tell in what order the letters from the character were written?

Positive and negative emotions are a universal experience. Brainstorm a list of feelings with the class: anger, fear, frustration, embarrassment, sadness, love, etc. Can students identify one instance of Leigh's feeling each of these emotions during the course of the story? What behaviors do Leigh's feelings cause him to display? What are the consequences of each behavior?

Main characters in good realistic fiction are always well-rounded, meaning they are neither perfectly good, nor totally bad. What instances can students list to show readers that Leigh has both good qualities and faults? Why is it important that the character be displayed this way?

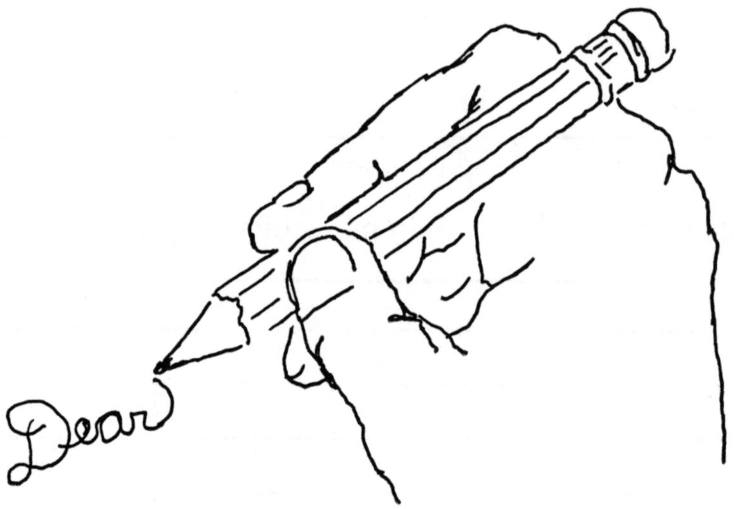

# Summer of the Swans

## *by Betsy Byars*

Fourteen-year-old Sara deals with many issues: her changing adolescent moods and body, sibling problems, and difficulty dealing with her aunt as a guardian. She feels misunderstood and longs for her absentee father. Perhaps one of her most frustrating issues, however, is her alternating feelings of frustration with and love for her mentally retarded brother.

***About the author:***

Betsy Byars is a popular and award-winning author of books for young people. She is probably best known for her skill and perception in understanding the problems children face. Her fiction books frequently deal with difficult social issues. *Summer of the Swans* won the 1970 John Newbery Medal.

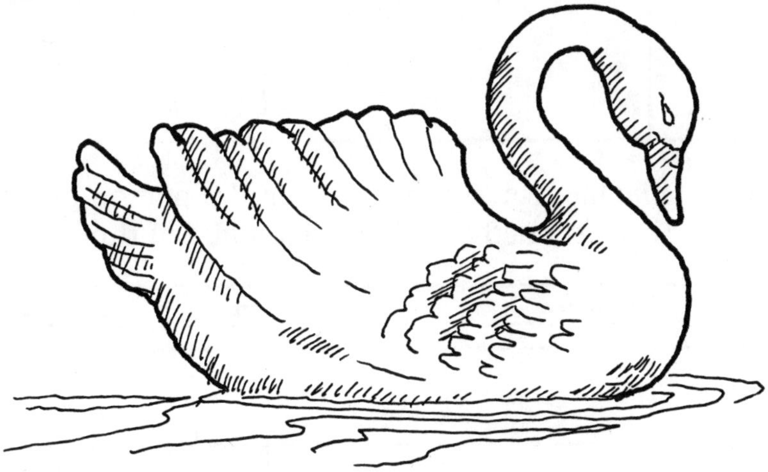

Byars, Betsy. *Summer of the Swans*. New York: Viking Press, 1970.

# Fears

Fears sometimes make us unable to look at things as they really are. Our fears often make circumstances seem much worse than they really are. When that happens, we often have trouble making wise decisions or staying calm enough to solve our problems.

Think of some events in the story that caused various characters to feel fear. Then think about what it was that each character feared was happening or was going to happen. Is that what really *did* happen?

| EVENT | CHARACTER/FEAR | WHAT *REALLY* HAPPENED? |
|---|---|---|
| 1. Wanda wanted to ride Frank's motor scooter. | Aunt Willie feared Wanda would break her neck. | |
| | | |
| | | |

Think about your *own* life. Have you ever feared a person or event and later discovered that everything turned out fine? List some of those times:

| EVENT | MY FEAR | WHAT *REALLY* HAPPENED? |
|---|---|---|
| | | |
| | | |
| | | |

Byars, Betsy. *Summer of the Swans*. New York: Viking Press, 1970.

# Yuck Thoughts

Yuck thoughts get us into trouble. Sometimes we don't realize that things we believe first become our thoughts, then our feelings, then . . . oops! . . . our behavior. Recognizing "yuck thoughts" helps us change beliefs that can get us in trouble.

Fill out the chart below with examples from *Summer of the Swans* and from your own life.

| "YUCK" Thought | What's really happening here? | Example in the story: | How did the thinking influence a character's behavior? | An example of "yuck thinking" in my own life: |
|---|---|---|---|---|
| Jumping to conclusions | Making a judgment or decision without knowing the whole story. | | | |
| "All of 'em and everybody": generalizations | Giving nothing/ no one a chance; deciding everyone/ thing in a certain group is a certain way. Ex.: "All boys are . . . All girls are . . ." | | | |
| Spotlighting the flaws | Looking at only the negatives in a situation, another person, or yourself. | | | |
| "Crystal ball thoughts": mind-reading | Being very sure you know what someone else must be thinking. Ex: "I'm sure she thought . . . I know exactly what he thinks . . ." | | | |

Byars, Betsy. *Summer of the Swans.* New York: Viking Press, 1970.

## Setting Priorities:

# First Things First!

Sara's mood changes a lot. One minute she likes something (like her orange sneakers), and the next minute she doesn't. She is dissatisfied with many things. Name some of them: ______________________________

______________________________________________

______________________________________________

What are some things you are dissatisfied with in your life? __________

______________________________________________

______________________________________________

The day Charlie disappeared, Sara figured out that she had some priorities. Charlie was more important to her than all of the other things that had bothered her. What are some priorities in your life, things that are more important than anything else that bothers you?

| 1. |
|---|
| 2. |
| 3. |
| 4. |
| 5. |

Byars, Betsy. *Summer of the Swans.* New York: Viking Press, 1970.

## *Other Things to Do with*

# Summer of the Swans

*Summer of the Swans* deals with a number of issues: Sara's changing moods in adolescence, her feelings toward an absentee father, her changing body, her envy of her older sister, and her acceptance of her mentally retarded brother. Have students brainstorm the issues Sara is confronting. Ask them to research in the library to make a list of nonfiction books that would help Sara deal with her problems if she were a real person.

Select several books that deal with the topic of mental retardation. *Welcome Home, Jellybean* (Shyer, Marlene Fanta. New York: Scribner, 1987) and *All Together Now* (Bridgers, Sue Ellen. New York: Knopf, 1979) are two examples. Have students compare Sara's experience and feelings with those of a character in another book dealing with similar pressures.

Sara often tolerates Aunt Willie, but does not often agree with her. She shows many signs of not understanding why Aunt Willie makes the decisions she does, and Aunt Willie does not seem to understand Sara. Have one group of students write Aunt Willie a letter from Sara outlining her frustrations and the reasons for them. Have another group of students write Sara a letter from Aunt Willie outlining her frustrations and reasons for her decisions. Role play a situation in which Aunt Willie and Sara are able to work through and agree upon one of the situations in the book. Stress the idea of a win-win solution, in which both characters are giving a bit to the other's point of view, both feel satisfied with the solution, and neither is completely giving in to the other's demands.

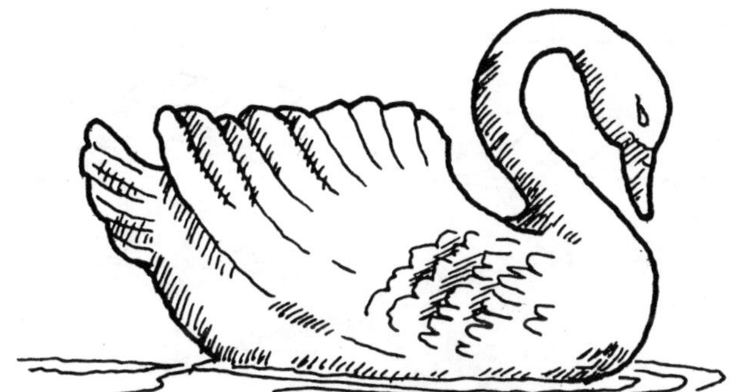

# Bridge to Terabithia

## *by Katherine Paterson*

*Bridge to Terabithia* is the story of two young people, Jess and Leslie, who become fast and firm friends despite their many differences. They learn to overcome prejudice and accept each other, building both a bridge of understanding and a secret fantasy kingdom they call Terabithia. Leslie's unexpected death launches a torrent of feeling inside Jess as he struggles to understand the meaning of his friendship and acceptance of its loss.

***About the author:***

Katherine Paterson is a highly acclaimed author of books for young people. She frequently writes about social issues that concern this age group. She has twice won both the John Newbery Medal and the National Book Award. *Bridge to Terabithia* is the 1978 John Newbery Medal winner.

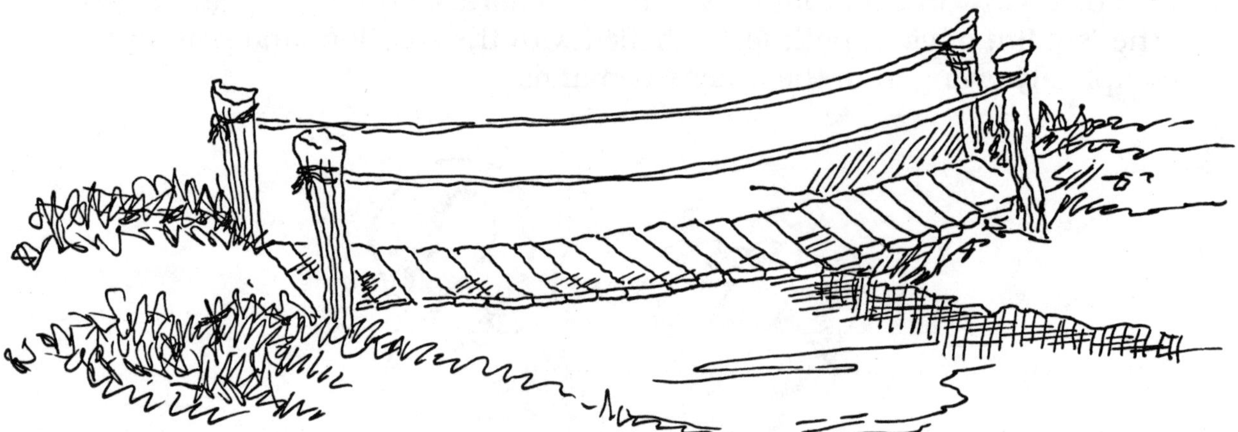

Paterson, Katherine. *Bridge to Terabithia.* New York: HarperCollins, 1977.

# Bridging Differences

Jess Aarons and Leslie Burke were from very different backgrounds. What differences did you note in the story?

| **Area of Differences:** | **Jess's Family's Ideas/Beliefs/Values** | **Leslie's Family's Ideas/Beliefs/Values** |
|---|---|---|
| Education | | |
| Money | | |
| Religion | | |
| Ideas about "how boys should be" and "how girls should be" | | |
| Parent-child relationships | | |
| Other differences | | |

Despite their differences, Jess and Leslie became very close friends. What qualities can you list that you feel helped them to overcome their differences?

___

___

___

Have you ever had a friend who came from a very different background than yours? List your differences. Think about the things that made the two of you able to be friends in spite of your differences:

___

___

___

Paterson, Katherine. *Bridge to Terabithia.* New York: HarperCollins, 1977.

# Learning to Say *Good-bye*

Jess was finally able to deal with Leslie's death with strength and courage. Before he was able to do so, however, he had to struggle with many painful emotions. Write some examples in the story concerning the emotions Jess felt:

| | |
|---|---|
| **Denial:** not wanting to believe the truth | |
| **Anger** at knowing the truth | |
| **Bargaining** in hopes of changing reality | |
| **Depression** and hopeless feelings of loss | |
| **Acceptance** | |

Jess at last realized some of the gifts that Leslie had given him just through sharing her life with him. What are some of the reasons Jess was glad he had known Leslie?

______________________________________________

______________________________________________

______________________________________________

______________________________________________

______________________________________________

## *To Think About:*

Have you ever had a loss? Would you have given up knowing that person, animal, or thing rather than have to face losing them? Are there reasons you are glad you did have this friendship or relationship in spite of the loss?

Paterson, Katherine. *Bridge to Terabithia.* New York: HarperCollins, 1977.

## More Ideas for

# Bridge to Terabithia

Leslie had to deal with much unfair thinking in regard to "how girls should be." Jess was surprised to realize that he had some prejudices of his own. What prejudices by other characters were evident in the story? Brainstorm stereotypes in our culture. Have students research to list successful people who have overcome the stereotypes of society. Have students look for examples of stereotypical thinking in advertisements and other media. Examine career books and informational science books. Can stereotypes be found in the text or in the illustrations?

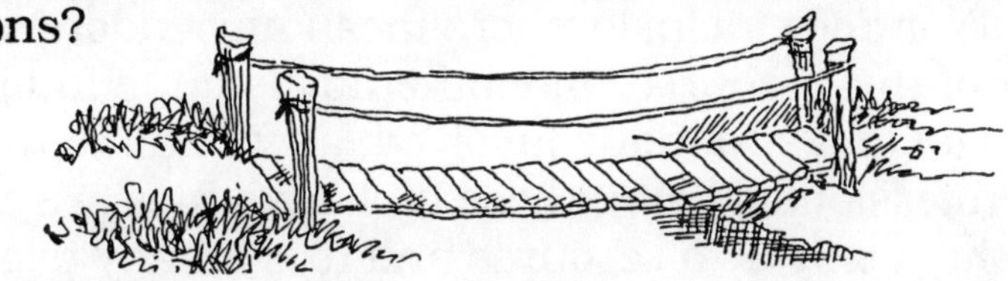

Leslie's family had decided they were "too hung up on money and success." They moved to a rural environment and made material sacrifices to try to figure out their true values. Have students examine advertisements to understand the types of messages often sent out to our culture. Have students look for the following types of messages:

Wealth and Success Message *(You are not a success unless you look wealthy and use this product!)*
So You Want to Be Glamorous! *(Women should be glamorous . . . but they can't do it without this product!)*
Athletic/Macho Message *(Healthy people are athletic . . . just like the pros . . . but you have to use the right product to be a pro!)*
Romance Message *(You are nothing without romance in your life . . . and you won't have it unless you use this product!)*
Everyone Uses It Message *(You want to keep up with everyone else, don't you? Well, everyone who is anyone uses this product!)*

Discuss the products the ads are selling. Are they really able to "magically" make these things happen? What messages and values are never promoted in advertisements? Have students count the number of "value messages" sent by advertisers in one evening of prime-time television. Is it sometimes hard to know our own values when we receive so many messages like this from the media?

# *Books for the Healing:*
# BIBLIOGRAPHIES

The following section is designed to give you a resource of available materials on a wide range of topics and for the wide range of maturity apparent at the middle school level. Matching just the right book to the right child is critically important, and for this reason each bibliographic entry is annotated, giving you insight into the sex and ages of main characters, as well as specific information on the plot and theme.

The bibliographies are not complete, but are rather intended only as a well-rounded aid to you. Nor does inclusion here mean any endorsement by the author or publisher of this resource. Bibliotherapy is quite individual and is unique to the person(s) and situations involved, as well as to the cultural mores of a locale. Professionals using these bibliographies are highly encouraged to use them only as a resource and to read any books under consideration before recommending them or using them in a classroom situation. It is also highly recommended that follow-up in the form of group or one-on-one discussion be utilized when either assigning or recommending books about problems to kids with problems. Bibliotherapy **cannot** be used in a clinical sense, nor can it take the place of counseling.

Listed below are the categories (subjects) by which this bibliography is organized.

- Abuse
- Adoption
- Aging and Relationships with the Elderly
- Death and Dying
- Divorce
- Drug and Alcohol Abuse
- Ethnic/Cultural Differences
- Family Life
- Fears
- Foster Children
- Growing Up
- Homelessness
- Illness
- Learning Disabilities
- Mental and Emotional Disabilities
- Peers: Problems and Pressures
- Physical Disabilities
- Prejudice
- Religious Differences
- Runaways
- School Life
- Sexuality and Sexual Stereotypes
- Stepfamilies
- Values and Ethics

# ABUSE

**Bawden, Nina. *Squib.* New York: Lothrop, Lee, & Shepard, 1982.**
Twelve-year-old Kate is searching for a missing younger brother. Her search leads her to a withdrawn little boy living with abusive relatives.

**Byars, Betsy. *Cracker Jackson.* New York: Viking Kestral, 1985.**
When Cracker Jackson learns that his adored babysitter is a victim of wife abuse, he sets off on a mission to get her and her baby into a home for battered women.

**Holman, Felice. *Slake's Limbo.* New York: Scribner, 1974.**
Thirteen-year-old Aremis runs away to the New York subways in an attempt to escape school and his abusive home.

# ADOPTION

**Howard, Ellen. *Her Own Song.* New York: Atheneum, 1988.**
Mellie must deal not only with the jibes of her classmates at being adopted, but with the loneliness that stems from her adopted mother's death.

**Neufield, John. *Edgar Allan.* New York: S. G. Phillips, 1968.**
Edgar is black and adopted by a white family. This is the story of the reactions by both family and community.

## Nonfiction

**Krementz, Jill. *How It Feels to Be Adopted.* New York: Knopf, 1982.**
A discussion of adoption from the perspective of nineteen adopted children of various ages.

# AGING AND RELATIONSHIPS WITH THE ELDERLY

**Clifford, Eth.** ***The Rocking Chair Rebellion.*** **Boston: Houghton Mifflin, 1978.**
Fourteen-year-old Opie finds herself enmeshed in the concerns of the elderly when she volunteers at a nursing home.

**Magorian, Michelle.** ***Goodnight, Mister Tom.*** **New York: Harper, 1986.**
A powerful story about a boy placed with a grumpy old man during the evacuation of London during World War II. This story deals with abuse, friendship, and kindness.

**Mazer, Norma Fox.** ***A Figure of Speech.*** **New York: Delacorte Press, 1973.**
Jenny is shocked to learn of her family's plans to move Grandpa into a home for the aged in order to make room for her older brother.

**Myers, Walter Dean.** ***Won't Know Till I Get There.*** **New York: Viking, 1982.**
Thirteen-year-old Earl and fourteen-year-old Steve find themselves sentenced to "volunteer" at a nursing home after an act of delinquency. This book tells the story of their growing awareness and compassion for the elderly as individuals.

**Taylor, Theodore.** ***The Cay.*** **Garden City, New York: Doubleday, 1969.**
A blind white boy and an old black man learn to depend on and respect each other when they find themselves shipwrecked on a Caribbean island.

**Voigt, Cynthia.** ***Dicey's Song.*** **New York: Atheneum, 1982.**
A sequel to *Homecoming,* this story focuses on the relationship of four abandoned children and the grandmother who has taken them in, as well as fourteen-year-old Dicey's struggle to let go of her responsibility and give herself room to grow.

## Nonfiction

**Frank, Julia.** ***Alzheimer's Disease: the Silent Epidemic.*** **Minneapolis, MN: Lerner Publications, 1985.**

# DEATH AND DYING

**Cleaver, Vera and Bill. *Grover.* Philadelphia: Lippincott, 1970.**
Grover must struggle to accept the suicide of his mother, who had cancer. Receiving no help from his grief-stricken father and suffering silently, he must learn to help himself.

**Greene, Constance. *Beat the Turtle Drum.* New York: Viking, 1976.**
Thirteen-year-old Kate deals with the loss and guilt attached to the accidental death of her younger sister.

**Hermes, Patricia. *You Shouldn't Have to Say Good-bye.* San Diego: Harcourt Brace Jovanovich, 1982.**
Thirteen-year-old Sarah must learn to cope with her mother's cancer and finally, with her death.

**Little, Jean. *Mama's Going to Buy You a Mockingbird.* New York: Viking Kestral, 1984.**
Eleven-year-old Jeremy must come to terms with his father's dying and his own compassion toward others.

**Lowry, Lois. *A Summer to Die.* Boston: Houghton Mifflin, 1977.**
Thirteen-year-old Meg has always been jealous of her beautiful older sister, Molly, and resentful of wearing her hand-me-downs. Meg has much to face in dealing with Molly's leukemia.

**Paterson, Katherine. *Bridge to Terabithia.* New York: HarperCollins, 1977.**
Although the theme of this story focuses on the death of a young girl, many other issues are thoughtfully approached: socioeconomic differences, religious differences, educational values, conscience, and what friendship means in all of these things.

**Smith, Doris B. *A Taste of Blackberries.* New York: HarperCollins, 1973.**
A young boy comes to terms with the death of his best friend who died as a result of an allergic reaction to bee stings.

## Nonfiction

**Krementz, Jill. *How It Feels When a Parent Dies.* New York: Knopf, 1981.**

**LeShan, Eda J. *Learning to Say Good-bye: When a Parent Dies.* New York: MacMillan, 1976.**

# DIVORCE

**Blume, Judy.** ***It's Not the End of the World.*** **Scarsdale, NY: Bradbury Press, 1972.**
Karen is traumatized by the development of her parents' impending divorce. It takes a frightening event for her to realize that even the nicest people sometimes just can't be married to each other.

**Cleary, Beverly.** ***Dear Mr. Henshaw.*** **New York: Dell, 1983.**
The letters and diary of a young boy, Leigh Botts, trace his struggle to cope with the divorce of his parents and the alienation he feels at school.

**Conrad, Pam.** ***Holding Me Here.*** **New York: Harper & Row, 1986.**
Fourteen-year-old Robin decides to take matters into her own hands when she learns that her mother's new boarder has abandoned her family. Believing "families should be together," she sets out to make this so, unaware that the woman has been abused. This is a story of divorce, conscience, and the invasion of privacy.

**Danziger, Paula.** ***The Divorce Express.*** **New York: Delacorte Press, 1982.**
Fourteen-year-old Phoebe is shuttled back and forth each weekend on "The Divorce Express," a bus that seems filled with children traveling between separated parents. This is the story of Phoebe's courage in learning to cope with her difficult experience.

**Fox, Paula.** ***The Moonlight Man.*** **New York: Bradbury Press, 1986.**
Fifteen-year-old Catherine has never fully accepted the divorce of her parents years before. However, an extended vacation with her father forces her to see and accept both him and the finality of the divorce.

**Kropp, Paul.** ***Moonkid and Liberty.*** **Boston: Little, Brown, & Co., 1990.**
Libby and Ian (high school students) are faced with a choice when their absent mother suddenly decides she'd like them to leave their father's home and live with her.

## Nonfiction

**Krementz, Jill.** ***How It Feels When Parents Divorce.*** **New York: Knopf, 1984.**

**See Also:** GROWING UP ***(Hatchet).***

# DRUG/ALCOHOL ABUSE

**Childress, Alice.** ***A Hero Ain't Nothing but a Sandwich.*** **New York: Coward, McCann, & Geoghegan, 1973.**
The story of a thirteen-year-old boy hooked on heroin, told from the viewpoints of the many people involved in his life.

**Myers, Walter Dean.** ***Fast Sam, Cool Clyde and Stuff.*** **New York: Viking, 1975.**
"Stuff" and his gang try to help a former friend, a drug addict. Stuff realizes the easiest thing to do would be to walk away, but his conscience won't let him.

## *Nonfiction*

**Hyde, Margaret.** ***Alcohol: Uses and Abuses.*** **Hillside, NJ: Enslow Publishers, 1988.**

**—.** ***Know about Drugs.*** **New York: Walker, 1990.**

**Rosenberg, Maxine.** ***Not My Family: Sharing the Truth about Alcoholism.*** **New York: Bradbury Press, 1988.**

**Stwertka, Eve and Albert.** ***Marijuana.*** **New York: F. Watts, 1986.**

**See Also:** GROWING UP ***(Up a Road Slowly).***

# ETHNIC/CULTURAL DIFFERENCES

**Clifford, Eth.** ***The Remembering Box.*** **Boston: Houghton Mifflin, 1985.**
This short novel concerns Joshua and his Jewish grandmother, whose habit is to spend the Sabbath opening the "remembering box" and discussing the treasures inside.

**Gilson, Jamie.** ***Hello, My Name Is Scrambled Eggs.*** **New York: Lothrop, Lee, & Shepard, 1985.**
Harvey sets out to Americanize twelve-year-old Tuan, a Vietnamese immigrant, and is himself educated in the process.

**Hamilton, Virginia.** ***M.C. Higgins the Great.*** **New York: Macmillan, 1974.**
The story of a thirteen-year-old black boy in rural Ohio is also the story of choices and responsibility.

**Lampman, Evelyn Sibley.** ***The Potlatch Family.*** **New York: Atheneum, 1976.**
Fourteen-year-old Plum Longor, a Chinook girl, grows from shame of her heritage to pride and learns that she, too, has prejudices.

**Lasky, Kathryn.** ***The Night Journey.*** **New York: F. Warne, 1986.**
Rachel learns of the persecution of the Jews in Czarist Russia in 1900 from her great-grandmother, who survived the experience.

**Lord, Bette Bao.** ***In the Year of the Boar and Jackie Robinson.*** **New York: Harper & Row, 1984.**
Set in Brooklyn in 1947, this is the story of a young Chinese girl's struggle to "begin again."

**Mohr, Nicholasa.** ***Going Home.*** **New York: Dial, 1986.**
Eleven-year-old Felita was born in New York, but her family is Puerto Rican. In this novel, Felita learns about the many forms of discrimination and the reader gains insight into Puerto Rican culture.

**Sneve, Virginia Driving Hawk.** ***When Thunders Spoke.*** **New York: Holiday, 1974.**
Norman Two Bull, a young Sioux boy, finds his identity and legacy through his grandfather despite the more modern views of his mother.

**Yarbrough, Camille.** ***The Shimmershine Queens.*** **New York: Putnam, 1989.**
Fifth grader Angie learns from an elderly relative the beauty of "inner glow" after enduring the taunts of her classmates because her skin is so dark.

**See Also:** RELIGIOUS DIFFERENCES, PREJUDICE.

# FAMILY LIFE

**Burch, Robert.** ***Queenie Peavy.*** **New York: Viking Press, 1966.**
Stubborn thirteen-year-old Queenie carries a chip on her shoulder to fend off attacks by her peers about her father, who is in jail. Queenie must come to terms with the truth of who her father is, as well as her own sense of responsibility.

**Byars, Betsy. *The Two-Thousand-Pound Goldfish.* New York: Harper & Row, 1982.**
Warren misses his absent mother and spends a good deal of time fantasizing about her, but Warren's mother is much too wrapped up in her radical underground movement to think of the child she has contacted only once in five years.

**Fine, Anne. *My War with Goggle-Eyes.* Boston: Little, Brown, & Co., 1989.**
Kitty resists the friendship of her mother's new boyfriend and is particularly displeased with his political views.

**Fox, Paula. *Blowfish Live in the Sea.* Englewood Cliffs, NJ: Bradbury Press, 1970.**
Thirteen-year-old Carrie struggles to help her nineteen-year-old half brother, Ben, a college dropout. Ben is disillusioned with his father and the two of them find out together the problems he really has. A story of acceptance and choices.

**Hamilton, Virginia. *A Little Love.* New York: Philomel, 1984.**
Sheema, a black teenager, feels abandoned and alone despite being raised by loving grandparents following the death of her mother and desertion of her father. In her quest for the father who does not want her, she comes to terms with reality and to understand what really matters in her life.

**Kerr, M. E. *Dinky Hocker Shoots Smack.* New York: Harper, 1972, 1989.**
Dinky is ignored by her socialite mother, who is on a crusade to cure the drug addicts in town. Dinky's desperate need for a caring mother is reflected in her rebellion.

**Klein, Norma. *Mom, the Wolfman and Me.* New York: Avon, 1976.**
Twelve-year-old Brett has lived a carefree casual life with her never-been-married mother. When her mother decides to marry Theo, Brett struggles to overcome her anger, feelings of rejection, and fear of change.

**Nelson, Theresa. *The 25 Cent Miracle.* New York: Bradbury Press, 1986.**
This book portrays the relationship of a widowed father and his spirited daughter, as well as the problems encountered when true feelings cannot be explored.

**Paterson, Katherine. *Jacob Have I Loved.* New York: Crowell, 1980.**
Louise tells the story of her relationship with her beautiful selfish twin, Caroline, from the early days of resentment and jealousy through the maturity of the days when Louise finds her own place in life and is ready for reconciliation.

**Stevenson, Laura. *Happily after All.* Boston: Houghton Mifflin, 1990.**
Becca's lifestyle changes drastically following the death of her father when she moves from California to Vermont to live with the mother she does not know. Becca learns that many of her preconceptions about her mother were not true.

**Voigt, Cynthia. *Building Blocks.* New York: Atheneum, 1984.**
Brann gains a new understanding of a father he has no respect for when he is transported into a fantasy world where his ten-year-old father is his friend.

**Wojciechowska, Maia. *Hey, What's Wrong With This One?* New York: Harper & Row, 1969.**
This humorous book deals with the efforts of three brothers to find a wife for their widowed father.

# FEARS

**Wallace, Bill. *A Dog Called Kitty.* New York: Holiday, 1980.**
This is the story of the struggle of a young boy to overcome his deep fear of dogs, which is based on an early traumatic experience.

**See Also:** GROWING UP ***(Call It Courage).***

# FOSTER CHILDREN

**Angell, Judie. *Tina Gogo.* Scarsdale, NY: Bradbury Press, 1978.**
Eleven-year-old Tina is a mistrustful foster child with problems. Tina's friendship with a "typical" girl and her family leads to a startling growth process.

**Byars, Betsy. *The Pinballs.* New York: Harper & Row, 1977.**
Three foster children with varied backgrounds have common ground. All feel that they are "pinballs," being knocked about from place to place. This is the story of their courage in deciding that they do indeed have choices in life.

**Paterson, Katherine. *The Great Gilly Hopkins.* New York: Crowell, 1978.**
Gilly's life has been filled with pain, abandonment, and mistrust. As a foster child, she is incorrigible and tough. This is the story of Gilly's road to compassion and responsibility for her own actions.

# GROWING UP

**Hunt, Irene. *Up a Road Slowly.* Chicago: Follett, 1966.**
This book tells Julie's story from her mother's death until her high school graduation ten years later. Woven throughout the book are the topics of parental relations, adolescent concerns, adult irresponsibility, and alcoholism.

**Miles, Betty. *The Trouble with Thirteen.* New York: Knopf, 1979.**
Annie and Rachel are twelve-year-olds when they learn how fast one sometimes has to grow up. Annie must adjust to losing Rachel when Rachel's parents divorce and she moves away.

**Paulsen, Gary. *Hatchet.* New York: Bradbury Press, 1987.**
A young boy, confused over his parents' divorce and resentful at what he perceives as his mother's betrayal, finds himself the lone survivor of a plane crash in the wilderness. Only a hatchet and courage will see him through.

**Peck, Robert Newton. *A Day No Pigs Would Die.* New York: Knopf, 1974.**
The story deals with a boy's coming of age at thirteen. Set in Vermont's Shaker country during the 1920s, it explores a number of issues, primarily life and death.

**Sperry, Armstrong. *Call It Courage.* New York: Macmillan, 1971.**
Armstrong's book tells the story of a boy's struggle to overcome his greatest fear: he endures the taunts of his peers.

**See also:** VALUES AND ETHICS.

# HOMELESSNESS

**Carlson, Natalie Savage. *The Family under the Bridge.* New York: Harper & Row, 1958.**
Armand likes his carefree life as a Parisian hobo. He has no desire to assume the responsibility that accompanies commitment. When a homeless family takes over his "homestead" beneath a bridge, Armand must make new choices.

**Hahn, Mary Downing. *December Stillness.* New York: Clarion Books, 1988.**
Thirteen-year-old Kelly's interest is piqued by a disturbed, homeless Vietnam War veteran.

**Holman, Felice. *Secret City, U.S.A.* New York: Scribner's, 1990.**
Benno and his gang live amid the squalor of an inner city ghetto. Finding an abandoned house, they try to create a home.

**Spinelli, Jerry. *Maniac Magee.* Boston: Little, Brown, & Co., 1990.**
"Maniac Magee," orphaned at age three, endures eight painful years before deciding to run. The subsequent story meshes homelessness, illiteracy, and racial prejudice.

**Voigt, Cynthia. *The Homecoming.* New York: Fawcett Juniper, 1984.**
Thirteen-year-old Dicey's mother abandons the family, and Dicey realizes she must assume the role of a parent and find a home for herself, her sister, and her two brothers.

# ILLNESS

**Sachs, Marilyn. *The Bears' House.* New York: Dutton, 1987.**
When a ten-year-old's father leaves the family and her mother becomes ill, she tries desperately to take care of the family. Unable to do so, she endures fear and the taunts of her classmates, and retreats to a fantasy world.

## Nonfiction

**LeShan, Eda. *When a Parent Is Very Sick.* Boston: Joy Street Books, 1986.**

**See Also:** MENTAL AND EMOTIONAL DISABILITIES; PHYSICAL DISABILITIES.

# LEARNING DISABILITIES

**Cassedy, Sylvia. *M.E. & Morton.* New York: Crowell, 1987.**
M.E. (Mary Ellen) is an excellent student, but has difficulty overcoming her shame of her learning disabled brother.

**Greenwald, Sheila. *Will the Real Gertrude Hollings Please Stand Up?* Boston: Little, Brown, & Co., 1983.**
Eleven-year-old Gertrude is a perfectly capable young lady, although she is dyslexic. She finds herself in the position of having to deal with an overachieving cousin and realizes that she may be able to help him with a problem of his own.

**Hall, Lynn. *Just One Friend.* New York: Macmillan, 1985.**
This is the story of a learning disabled student's fear of mainstreaming.

**Pevsner, Stella. *Keep Stompin' Till the Music Stops.* New York: Seabury Press, 1977.**
Twelve-year-old Richard tries to come to terms with his dyslexia at the same time his great-grandfather asserts his own ability to live independently.

**Smith, Doris Buchanan. *Kelly's Creek.* New York: Crowell, 1975.**
Nine-year-old Kelly is aware that he is not like other children and not successful in school. Despite his learning disabilities, he finds success and friendship in other ways.

## Nonfiction

**Fisher, Gary, and Rhoda Woods Cummings. *The Survival Guide for Kids With LD.* Minneapolis, MN: Free Spirit Publishers, 1990.**

# MENTAL AND EMOTIONAL DISABILITIES

**Bridgers, Sue Ellen. *All Together Now.* New York: Knopf, 1979.**
A poignant story of twelve-year-old Casey who contracts polio and gains insight and maturity through her friendship with an adult retarded man.

**Brooks, Bruce.** ***The Moves Make the Man.*** **New York: Harper & Row, 1984.**
The boy narrating this story tells how the breakdown of his friend's mother very nearly proves his breakdown as well.

**Byars, Betsy.** ***The Summer of the Swans.*** **New York: Viking Press, 1970.**
The story of fourteen-year-old Sara who is struggling with adolescent moods and fears, as well as her relationship with a retarded brother.

**Cleaver, Vera and Bill.** ***Me Too.*** **Philadelphia: Lippincott, 1973.**
Lydia must learn to accept what she cannot change despite her valiant efforts to teach her retarded twin and make her acceptable in the eyes of her father.

**Lisle, Janet Taylor.** ***Afternoon of the Elves.*** **New York: Orchard Books, 1989.**
Nine-year-old Hillary lives in a stable happy home, but finds herself confused in her friendship with the highly imaginative twelve-year-old Sara-Kate. Sara-Kate is an outcast, poor, and failing in school. Hillary discovers that Sara-Kate is trying to care for her mentally ill mother alone.

**Riley, Jocelyn.** ***Only My Mouth Is Smiling.*** **New York: Morrow, 1982.**
Thirteen-year-old Merle increasingly realizes that her mother's erratic behavior is growing more out of control and that the family must have help.

**Shyer, Marlene Fanta.** ***Welcome Home, Jellybean.*** **New York: Scribner, 1978.**
This story is told by twelve-year-old Neil, who must face the problems caused by a retarded older sister home after years in an institution.

### Nonfiction

**Dinner, Sherry H.** ***Nothing to Be Ashamed Of: Growing up with Mental Illness in Your Family.*** **New York: Lothrop, Lee, & Shepard, 1989.**

## PEERS: PROBLEMS AND PRESSURES

**Blume, Judy.** ***Blubber.*** **New York: Bradbury Press, 1974.**
Ten-year-old Linda is overweight and must bear the cruel taunts of her classmates. An eye-opener about the ability of a strong leader to manipulate individuals.

**Burch, Robert.** ***King Kong and Other Poets.*** **New York: Viking Kestrel, 1986.**
Sixth-grader Andy reaches out to befriend the "new girl," Marilyn, and discovers that the qualities that make her seem so aloof and strange may spring from an unhappy background.

**Duncan, Lois.** ***Killing Mr. Griffin.*** **Boston: Little, Brown, & Co., 1978.**
This is a chilling story of peer pressure and guilt, revolving around five high school students and their plot to kidnap their loathed English teacher in an attempt to scare him.

**Estes, Eleanor.** ***The Hundred Dresses.*** **New York: Harcourt, Brace, Jovanovich, 1974.**
Wendy is from the "wrong side of town" and is taunted by her classmates about the "hundred dresses" she says she has.

**Fitzhugh, Louise.** ***Harriet the Spy.*** **New York: Harper & Row, 1964.**
Harriet's habit of recording her frank opinions about her friends in her notebook catches up with her when her classmates discover it.

**Mazer, Norma Fox.** ***Mrs. Fish, Ape, and Me, the Dump Queen.*** **New York: Dutton, 1980.**
Joyce struggles to hold her head up and face the world with dignity, despite the derision of her classmates concerning her guardian uncle, the manager of the town dump. The "crazy" school custodian provides an unexpected source of help.

**O'Connor, Jane.** ***Yours till Niagara Falls, Abby.*** **New York: Hastings House, 1979.**
Ten-year-old Abby feels it is the end of the world when she must be separated from her best friend for two months at camp.

**Robinson, Barbara.** ***The Best Christmas Pageant Ever.*** **New York: Harper & Row, 1972.**
An entire community learns quite a bit about making judgments when a family of children from the "wrong side of the tracks" decides to take over the church Christmas play. A heartwarming, humorous look at what happens when socioeconomic stratas cross.

**See Also:** VALUES AND ETHICS ***(Death Run)***; SCHOOL LIFE.

# PHYSICAL DISABILITIES

**Corcoran, Barbara. *A Dance to Still Music.* New York: Atheneum, 1974.**
Fourteen-year-old Margaret runs in fear from the idea of attending a school for the deaf and meeting new people in a new location.

**Garfield, James. *Follow My Leader.* New York: Viking Press, 1957.**
Eleven-year-old Jimmy finds himself blinded after an accident with a firecracker. This is the story of his acceptance of a disability and the circumstances surrounding it.

**Girion, Barbara. *A Handful of Stars.* New York: Scribner, 1981.**
High school sophomore Julie must learn to live with epileptic seizures.

**Howard, Ellen. *Circle of Giving.* New York: Atheneum, 1984.**
Margarite's world is changed when she meets Francie, a child with cerebral palsy. Francie's mother finds the problem difficult to cope with and views Francie as a burden.

**Howe, James. *A Night without Stars.* New York: Atheneum, 1983.**
Eleven-year-old Maria fears her heart surgery. It is "Monster Man," with horrible burn scars, who helps her face her fears.

**Little, Jean. *Mine for Keeps.* Boston: Little, Brown, & Co., 1962.**
Sally, a young girl with cerebral palsy, comes home after being in a school for the disabled. This is the story of her struggles to adapt and mainstream.

**Pollock, Penny. *Keeping It Secret.* New York: Putnam, 1982.**
Eleven-year-old Wisconsin faces problems when she changes schools, where none of the sixth graders know about her hearing impairment and hearing aid.

**Slote, Alfred. *Hang Tough, Paul Mather.* New York: Harper & Row, 1985.**
A young boy struggles with leukemia and his desire to continue playing baseball.

**Voigt, Cynthia. *Izzy, Willy-Nilly.* New York: Atheneum, 1986.**
A young girl loses her legs in an automobile accident and must cope with her own emotions, her mother's denial, and her friends' discomfort.

# PREJUDICE

**Taylor, Mildred. *The Friendship.* New York: Dial, 1987.**
A story of racial bigotry in Mississippi during the 1930s. The Logan children are caught up in the prejudice inherent in the Depression-era South and learn how quickly social attitudes can turn to violence.

**—. *Roll of Thunder, Hear My Cry.* New York: Dial, 1976.**
A black family in Mississippi during the Depression exhibits courage and pride in the face of harassment.

**See Also:** RELIGIOUS DIFFERENCES; ETHNIC/CULTURAL DIFFERENCES; SCHOOL LIFE ***(I Hate Being Gifted);*** LEARNING DISABILITIES; PHYSICAL DISABILITIES; MENTAL AND EMOTIONAL DISABILITIES; SEXUALITY/SEXUAL STEREOTYPES ***(Winning Kicker);*** RUNAWAYS ***(Maniac Magee).***

# RELIGIOUS DIFFERENCES

**Arrick, Fran. *Chernowitz!* New York: Bradbury Press, 1981.**
Ninth grader Bobby takes an aggressive stand against the bully that harasses a Jewish family.

**Neville, Emily. *Berries Goodman.* New York: HarperCollins Children's Books, 1975.**
This is the story of Berrie's friendship with a Jewish boy and the prejudice he sees in the world around him.

# RUNAWAYS

**Bulla, Clyde Robert. *The Cardboard Crown.* New York: Crowell, 1984.**
Eleven-year-old Adam helps Olivia, a frightened unhappy girl, run from her guardian aunt.

**Hughes, Dean. *Family Pose.* New York: Atheneum, 1989.**
Eleven-year-old David is stubborn and desperate when he runs away from an uncaring foster family. His friendship with a reformed alcoholic leads to self-discovery and a facing of reality.

**Spinelli, Jerry.** ***Maniac Magee.*** **Boston: Little, Brown, & Co., 1990.**
Magee spends eight unhappy years with relatives before taking off on his own. He deals with racial prejudice, illiteracy, and issues surrounding homelessness. This story is a little bit "tall tale," but still very thought-provoking.

# SCHOOL LIFE

**Bunting, Eve.** ***Our Sixth-Grade Sugar Babies.*** **New York: Lippincott, 1990.**
The sixth grade has been assigned the project of lugging about five pound bags of sugar to learn about parental responsibility. Vicki and her friend fear how this will make them appear to a particular seventh-grade boy.

**Conford, Ellen.** ***Dear Lovey Hart: I Am Desperate.*** **Boston: Little, Brown, & Co., 1975.**
Carrie is not only having "love life" problems of her own, but as the writer of an advice column in the school newspaper, she is finding that the problems addressed to her are often beyond her experience, and her advice sometimes causes disastrous results.

**Conford, Ellen.** ***Seven Days to a Brand-New Me.*** **Boston: Little, Brown, & Co., 1981.**
Self-help books are Maddy's answer to shyness, especially because she wants the attention of a particular boy. Maddy finds solace and insight through her mother and friends.

**Hermes, Patricia.** ***Friends Are Like That.*** **San Diego: Harcourt Brace Jovanovich, 1984.**
If thirteen-year-old Tracy drops her best friend who just doesn't fit in, she can join the most popular crowd at school.

**—.** ***I Hate Being Gifted.*** **New York: Putnam, 1990.**
KT deals with the peer problems that result form the label of "gifted."

**Sharmat, Marjorie Weiman.** ***Mysteriously Yours, Maggie Marmelstein.*** **New York: Harper & Row, 1982.**
Maggie is the mystery columnist for the school newspaper and learns the hard way that with power comes responsibility.

# SEXUALITY AND SEXUAL STEREOTYPES

**Adler, C. S. *The Once in a While Hero.* New York: Coward, McCann, & Geoghegan, 1982.**
Seventh grader Pat is confused about his own sexuality. The facts that his two best friends are girls and that he has long hair and a gentle disposition add to his confusion.

**Blume, Judy. *Are You There, God? It's Me, Margaret.* New York: Bradbury Press, 1970.**
Although this book is becoming a bit dated, it is still an excellent choice for girls who share Margaret's concern over physical maturation. Margaret is fearful that her breast size will not increase and that she will be the last to start menstruating.

**—. *Then Again, Maybe I Won't.* New York: Bradbury Press, 1971.**
Thirteen-year-old Tony is embarrassed by his physical maturation. He learns to accept this issue and to grow his own personal values.

**Donovan, John. *Remove Protective Coating a Little at a Time.* New York: Harper & Row, 1973.**
Fourteen-year-old Harry struggles to grow up physically and emotionally, while his mother is dealing with an emotional problem and he continues to have trouble communicating with his father. This book contains explicit sexual references.

**Dygard, Thomas J. *Winning Kicker.* New York: Morrow, 1978.**
This is the story of a girl who makes the high school football team as a place kicker and the crusty football coach who finds his attitudes challenged.

## Nonfiction

**Madaras, Lynda. *The What's Happening to My Body Book for Boys: A Growing Up Guide for Parents and Sons.* New York: New Market Press, 1995.**

**—. *The What's Happening to My Body Book for Girls: A Growing Up Guide for Parents and Daughters.* New York: New Market Press, 1995.**

# STEPFAMILIES

**Bawden, Nina. *The Outside Child.* New York: Lothrop, Lee, & Shepard, 1989.**
Thirteen-year-old Janie is startled when she learns that her absent widowed father has remarried and has two other children. She sets out on a quest to meet her half siblings and deals with the hostility of her stepmother.

**Bridgers, Sue Ellen. *Home before Dark.* New York: Knopf, 1976.**
Fourteen-year-old Stella views her family's settling down after years as a migrant family as positive. However, she must grow and overcome her reluctance to adapt to a new stepmother.

**Hahn, Mary Downing. *Wait till Helen Comes.* New York: Clarion Books, 1986.**
Although this book is a modern day ghost story, the very real issue of Molly and Michael's adjustment to a stepfamily is woven intricately into the plot.

**Park, Barbara. *My Mother Got Married (and Other Disasters).* New York: Knopf, 1989.**
Twelve-year-old Charlie angrily tells the story of his new adjustment to a stepfamily.

**Smith, Doris Buchanan. *The First Hard Times.* New York: Viking Press, 1983.**
Twelve-year-old Ancil has difficulty accepting her new stepfather. Her loyalties remain with her MIA father, whom she believes will someday return.

# VALUES AND ETHICS

**Bauer, Marion Dane. *On My Honor.* New York: Clarion Books, 1986.**
Joel tells no one of his best friend's drowning, trying to deny what has happened. A gripping story of choices and values.

**Byars, Betsy. *The Midnight Fox.* New York: Viking Press, 1968.**
Tommy must spend the summer with an aunt and uncle he is determined not to like. Confrontation occurs and values are realized when Tommy is determined to keep alive a renegade fox that his uncle is equally determined to kill.

**Fleischman, Sid. *The Whipping Boy.* New York: Greenwillow Books, 1986.**
The medieval prince in this short novel is much too precious to ever be spanked, so the king vents his frustration on Jeremy, a peasant. Both boys grow when an unusual circumstance allows the boys to reverse the roles.

**Fox, Paula. *One-Eyed Cat.* New York: Bradbury Press, 1984.**
Eleven-year-old Ned shoots the rifle he is forbidden to use, hitting something in the dark. The story of moral dilemma and conscience, this book also carries a subplot involving death and dying.

**Murphy, Jim. *Death Run.* New York: Clarion Books, 1982.**
Brian must deal with his conscience and peer pressure in regard to a terrible secret. He and three other boys are well aware that the death of a high school ball player was the result of a prank, not the accident it appears to be.

**Rawls, Wilson. *Where the Red Fern Grows.* New York: Doubleday, 1961.**
A story of growing up and values that touches on many issues: sacrifice, courage, work ethic, family, and death. This is the story of a ten-year-old Ozark mountain boy who scrimps, saves, and sacrifices for a pair of hounds.

**Wagner, Jane. *J.T.* New York: Dell, 1971.**
An inner-city black child is on the verge of becoming a delinquent in spite of his mother's best efforts. It is a one-eyed stray cat that finally reaches his sense of responsibility and caring.